Author's Note & Thanks

I had originally decided to go it alone when writing, editing, and designing the graphics for this book. However, come the final synopsis I have been very grateful for the support of several people. The final book cover was designed by my longest suffering friend, Chris Wheeler. His website and company can be found on the back page. Additionally, a colleague's partner was kind enough to professionally proofread the text and managed to pick up several errors.

Various other people have been gracious enough to read early versions of this text, and to lend me their thoughts. I am grateful for their time and expertise. This book is better for it.

Any remaining errors, of which I am sure there are many, are entirely my own. However, given the subject matter, I think a little human frailty is in keeping with the following pages. We are not machines. Whilst a machine may have written technically better prose, it would not have been able to extract the insights from interviewees that led to the content in the first place, nor synthesise the resulting information in the creative way that is unique to a human author.

I would like to thank Dr. Hamad Buamim for being kind enough to write the foreword, Kieran Gilmurray for writing the back cover endorsement, and Carl and Susie Ward for granting me access to Adobe InDesign. Finally, to the many interviewees who freely gave their time and insight in support of my original thesis, this work wouldn't exist without your generosity.

~ Contents ~

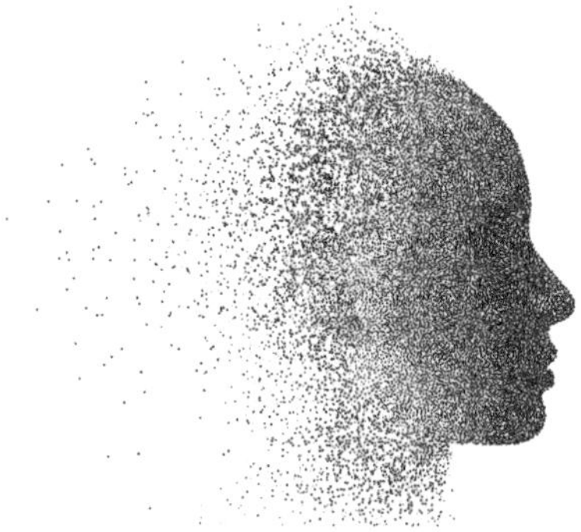

Foreword

"The difficulty lies not so much in developing new ideas as in escaping from old ones."

John Maynard Keynes

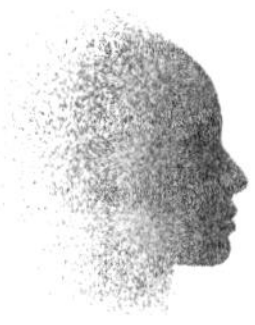

~ Foreword ~

I met David on the first day of our doctoral programme with Warwick University Business School back in 2018. I forget what we talked about now as we sat in the auditorium, contemplating the twists of fate that had led us to think that a DBA was a good idea! However, I remember from the earliest days of our friendship that David was fascinated by both technology and decision-making.

At the time, I was serving as the President of the Dubai Chamber of Commerce and an active board member for several large organisations. While every board I have sat on has had its own nuance, they have all operated as the nexus for high-stakes decisions related to the companies we were privileged to oversee.

Over the years, David and I got to know each other well, and I watched with interest as his research developed. In parallel, I witnessed firsthand the difficulty that organisations faced in striking a balance between rapidly advancing technology and human talent.

When the time came, I was a natural choice to be included in David's list of interviewees. We spoke at length about human decision-making, judgement, the role of technology, and the intricacies of corporate governance. Our discussion was wide-ranging and extended well beyond the allotted time. It was not a quick exchange of questions and answers but a two-way dialogue that explored his central themes. I was intrigued to see what David would do with the results.

Nearly 18 months later, I sat and listened as David presented his findings and articulated a first draft of the model that forms the central theme of this book. Although it was only a twenty-minute presentation, the content resonated strongly with me and the audience. By now, AI was front and centre in people's thoughts, and while David's model was not limited to any specific technology, it was clear that the discussion was highly topical, relevant, and timely.

As a time-constrained chairman and board member, I recognise many of David's themes. I appreciate the critical importance of human talent and value judgement, experience, and the ability to influence others. I also acknowledge that the world is changing rapidly, and that technology plays an increasingly significant role in organisational decision-making. With data democracy providing greater transparency than ever before, I actively encourage my executive teams to make better, data-driven decisions on behalf of the organisations they serve.

Automating lower-level, transactional decisions is a great way for busy executives to free up their time to focus on the decisions that really drive shareholder value.

While the following pages contain few absolutes, this book presents a model to frame the complex interplay between technology and talent. In a rapidly changing world, it serves as a useful reference for senior executives to consider one of the defining questions of our time: where should we deploy machines to support organisational decisions, and where should we prioritise human talent?

Dr. Hamad Buamim

President DMCC

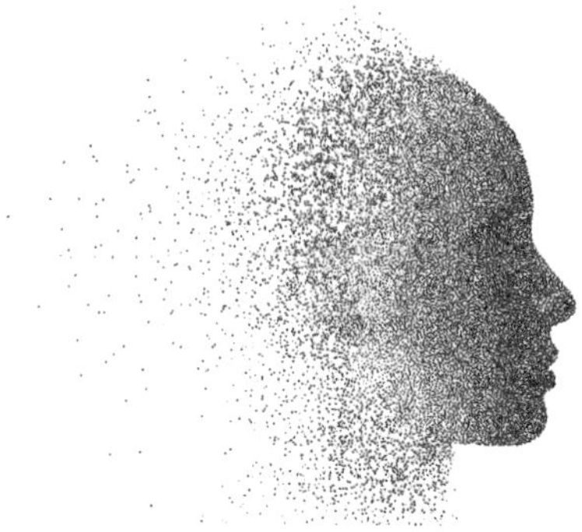

Navigating This Book

"Time is really the only capital that any human being has, and the only thing he can't afford to lose."

Thomas Edison

~ Navigating This Book ~

Technology looks set to transform our daily lives. Some commentators speculate that we are headed towards a dystopian future in which human productivity is all but replaced by machines, rendering human labour moot. Others point towards an unheralded period of prosperity in which human workers aided by machines transcend boundaries previously determined by our cognitive limitations.

Reality will likely fall somewhere between these two extremes. What is certain is that the world will soon look very different. As leaders, it is important to stay curious, prepare, and act. Being passive in the face of change is rarely a good strategy.

In a world where technology solutions emerge to answer questions before they've even formed in our minds, it is easy to lose sight of the delicate balance that needs to be struck. Despite the hyperbole surrounding technology, human talent still plays a critical role in the success of modern organisations.

Technology is unlikely to displace highly skilled professionals entirely. However, it will significantly disrupt businesses at a *task* level. Given that decision-making is one of the most recurring tasks in any organisation and critical to shareholder returns, it is perhaps surprising that more has not been written about organisational decision-making in the context of the current wave of technology. Certainly, limited practical advice exists to inform executives.

Certain decisions are undoubtedly well suited to machine intelligence's tireless and formulaic nature. Others require a mix of human judgement, experience, and, dare I say it, intuition. In the coming pages, we will explore a model that helps organisational leaders frame the debate and consider both human talent and technology.

This book is structured to be accessible to time-constrained executives. Chapter 2 provides a comprehensive but succinct overview of the model that serves as our central theme. The following chapters explore each element of the model in greater detail. As such, the book can be read in part, or front to back. The choice is yours.

The navigation aid below is designed to help you orient yourself and determine where to focus your reading. Enjoy!

Chapter 1. Introduction

Provides background narrative on organisational, human, and machine decision-making, and the rise of AI - framing the debate.

Chapter 2. A Model for Practice: Overview

Sets out a comprehensive summary of the model that forms the book's central theme.

Chapter 3. Background: Human Decision-Making

Explores the theory and practice behind human decision-making covering utility theory, heuristics, intuition, regret and System 1 and System 2 thinking. It's honestly not as hard work as I've just made it sound!

Chapter 4. Background: Machine Decision-Making

Considers the early history of artificial intelligence, the rapid acceleration of technology, and its likely impact on decision-making.

Chapter 5. Background: Organisational Decision-Making

In the context of human and machine decision-making, the chapter reviews the theory behind organisational design, agency theory, the role of the board, and the challenge of striking a balance between talent and automation.

Chapter 6. A Model for Practice

A succinct summary of the research that underpins this book and the associated model.

Chapter 7. A Model for Practice: Criticality of Data

Introduces the role of data in driving the automation of decision-making, introducing our two axes, data volume/complexity and data sufficiency.

Chapter 8. A Model for Practice: Automation Zone

Covers the first of three decision zones, highlighting the criticality of machines in dealing with data complexity and pioneering insight.

Chapter 9. A Model for Practice: Talent Zone

The second decision zone highlights the role of human talent in high-stakes organisational decision-making, highlighting the ability to creatively project the future and influence others.

Chapter 10. A Model for Practice: Grey Zone

An introduction to Grey Zone decision making - characterised by narrow use cases, questionable return on investment, and pilot proliferation.

Chapter 11. A Model for Practice: Accelerators

Introduces the drivers that will see machines increasingly encroach into human domains, highlighting the role of connected devices, synthetic data, digital operations, and machine learning.

Chapter 12. A Model for Practice: Accommodation & Resistance

A review of the various factors that will both accommodate and resist the progress of technology, including legislation, customer attitudes, and regulatory/professional bodies.

Chapter 13. A Look to the Future

Concluding comments and a look towards a dynamic future.

Annex I. Application in Practice

A short practical guide to using the proffered model for practice in a workshop setting.

Annex II. Writing & Publishing in the Age of AI

Given the nature of the book, it would have felt somewhat remiss not to write a short account of my experiences both writing and self-publishing in light of recent advances in technology.

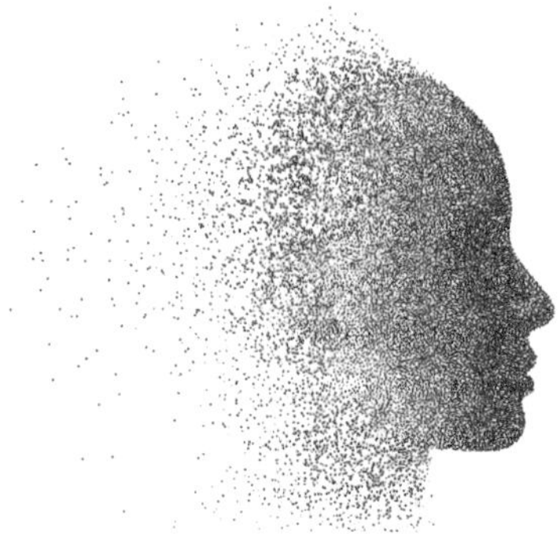

Chapter 1

Introduction

"At a child's birth, if a mother could ask a fairy godmother to endow it with the most useful gift, that gift would be curiosity."

Eleanor Roosevelt

~ Introduction ~

Over my 47 years, I have watched with fascination as technology has transformed almost every aspect of our daily lives. At university, I first encountered the Internet and email, and later worked at the company that invented and patented SMS text messaging. I have spent my career negotiating technology contracts from both sides of the table, giving me a front-row seat as the world has undergone digital transformation. I was at the forefront as we transitioned from physical infrastructure to the public cloud, witnessed the rise of the smartphone, and observed with fascination as data exploded fuelled by the rapid growth of connected devices.

I'm naturally curious, and my doctorate with the University of Warwick Business School was an ideal opportunity to exercise that curiosity with *purpose*. When you are immersed in a busy day job, it can be difficult to abstract yourself long enough to really observe and reflect upon what is going on around you. It is, however, a fascinating time to be alive.

As luck would have it, I was in the final stages of my doctorate when Generative Artificial Intelligence (GAI) began to capture public interest, having spent four and a half years researching the impact of technology on the future of organisational decision-making. I sat my viva at a time when ChatGPT was still in its infancy but already beginning to make its presence felt. To me, it felt like validation of the questions I had been asking.

At the start of my programme in 2018, AI was limited to narrow use cases and high-tech industries. Skip forward a few years, and it has become mainstream.

That said, this book is not focused purely on AI. I am naturally sceptical about the labels attached to technology. Rebranding traditional technology can be highly lucrative in the eyes of investors and potential clients, and reality be damned. So, I tend to consider technology on its practical merits. After twenty-five years in commercial roles, I am almost impervious to hyperbole. To my mind, it makes little difference whether something is described as AI, intelligent automation, or otherwise. What matters is what the technology does and how it does it. So, whilst we will discuss AI in the following pages, for the large part, the principles outlined apply broadly across all forms of technology and automation.

Although I've always been very pro-technology, I have also been endlessly fascinated by people.

I have had the good fortune to lead reasonably large teams of people over the past twenty years. The one thing that you can always count on is that people will constantly surprise you, both positively and negatively. People are unpredictable in ways that technology is not.

I am convinced that both technology and talent are essential in the modern organisation. The question is how to strike an effective balance between the two.

The Rapid Acceleration of Technology

Artificial Intelligence is not a new phenomenon, having first been coined in 1956 by John McCarthy. For many years, however, it has felt like a distant promise. Expert systems dominated the landscape - expensive to build and laborious to code. While capable of some impressive feats, they were narrow in focus and almost entirely dependent on knowledge engineers prescribing responses to predetermined inputs.

In recent times, technology has advanced at an impressive speed. Ideas once confined to the pages of science fiction novels have become a reality. Self-driving vehicles are increasingly prevalent on our roads, autonomous weapons have changed the face of warfare, and intelligent machines have started to transform industry.

Until recently, such advances were limited to high-tech industries, and the associated feats, while impressive, were far from mainstream.

However, in November 2022, ChatGPT was launched on an unsuspecting public. Although adoption was not instantaneous, the take-up was rapid. OpenAI created a system capable of supporting a dizzying breadth of tasks in real-time. As ever, there were both sceptics and advocates in almost equal measure. However, regardless of which camp you sat in, and whether you knew it or not, a new era of Generative AI had been born.

Since then, an entire industry has been spawned, with ever-more-advanced versions of GAI being released. Such has been the impact of the technology that it is easy to forget that it is still only two years old!

Many solution providers have jumped on a lucrative bandwagon, rebranding legacy technology to capitalise on the furore. As a result, the market contains as much hyperbole as substance. Solutions are emerging from every direction, promising to reshape company fortunes and transform all aspects of the associated operations.

While some impressive technology has undoubtedly been developed, there is also a lot of snake oil. For business leaders, it is difficult to separate fact from fiction, know where to focus investment, and find a way through all the noise.

Balancing Technology & Talent

Despite the promise of technology enabled futures, organisational prosperity will not be determined by automation alone. Unless and until machines take over, organisations will continue to be run by people for the benefit of people.

The flip side of the technology debate, then, concerns how and where to deploy human talent to optimal effect. Organisations must remember and respect the unique capabilities that make us all human. Striking an effective balance between technology and human talent will become increasingly existential. Those who succeed will thrive, while those who don't will struggle to remain relevant.

The situation will be dynamic. The world will continue to change quickly and unpredictably, but the fundamental challenge of balancing technology and talent will remain a constant. Despite myself, I cannot help but return to the words of Trudeau, who famously stated, 'the pace of change has never been this fast, yet it will never be this slow again.'[1] This statement feels more apt than ever before.

Exponential Growth

Despite GAI's impact in recent months, the current offerings are a mere taste of what's to come. The next wave of innovation is going to blow people's minds! Quantum computing, Artificial General Intelligence, and other yet unimagined technologies will make the last few years feel like a mere ripple in the face of the tidal wave of change that is headed our way.

A challenge in envisioning the future is that humans struggle to think exponentially. We tend to think in linear terms, viewing progress as a series of incremental improvements based on past developments. However, technology progresses exponentially, not linearly.

Although it is little more than a proxy, Moore's Law suggests that computing power will double every two years. We all know this; it has been hammered into us. But how many of us truly understand the implications of compound exponential growth?

I offer two well-cited examples to reinforce this point. Indulge me, please, by grabbing a piece of paper.

Now, fold it as many times as you can. You should get to around six or seven folds, depending on the thickness of the paper you started with.

---

1 Justin Trudeau's Davos address in full. https://www.weforum.org/agenda/2018/01/pm-keynote-remarks-for-world-economic-forum-2018/: World Economic Forum.

You've taken something that started at 0.1mm and doubled it six or seven times to create a lump of pulp with a height of around 6.4mm - 12.8mm.

Question for you.

If it were physically possible, how many times would you need to fold a piece of paper to reach the moon? The moon is approximately 384,000 kilometres away from Earth, give or take.

Note: I thought the answer would be in the thousands when asked this question.

The reality, however, is that it is a mere 42 times. 42!

That is the power of exponential growth. Continuing to double anything results in unfathomably large numbers in double-quick time.

I offer one more example. If you were to place a single grain of rice on the first square of a chessboard and double it on each subsequent square, how many grains of rice would you have by the time you reach the end of the board? This one may test your math skills and the number of digits on your calculator. A chessboard, of course, has 64 squares.

The answer is 18,466,744,073,709,551,615 grains. That is just shy of eighteen and a half quintillion grains of rice!

Why have I risked labouring this point? Simply because the world has already changed rapidly, but technology's exponential progress is going to continue unabated. From this point forward, you will need an active imagination to project the future.

Preparing to Act

Over the next decade, the future is likely to be terrifying and fascinating in almost equal measure. That said, the purpose of this book is not to descend into a monologue about hopes and fears. I will leave it to others to comment on such matters. Whether technology should be feared or heralded is an interesting question to consider over a beer, but one that has limited practical value to organisational leaders. We need to take a far more grounded view based on merit.

The important point, however, is that if leaders restrict themselves to looking at today's technology, they risk being blindsided by what comes next - spending a lot of money in the process. After working in corporate environments for over twenty years, I have observed a tendency for organisations to be perpetually behind the curve. I used to describe the phenomena as looking at *yesterday's technology today*. In such a fast-paced world, leaders need to consider *tomorrow's technology today*.

In the following pages, I offer practical guidance on how to tackle the fundamental challenge facing organisational leaders: where to deploy technology and where to double down on human talent. This is, however, a huge question.

Tasks as a Unit of Analysis

Despite the rhetoric, it is unlikely that industries will see a wholesale disruption of jobs. Most white-collar workers perform a wide range of tasks, not all of which are necessarily related to one another. This makes it very challenging to displace an entire person. Few high-level jobs will be entirely automated in the near future (although there will be exceptions).

Technology will disrupt at the *task* level. Elements of existing roles will be augmented or displaced by increasingly sophisticated technology. Thus, when considering the future of technology within an organisational context, we should use *tasks* as our unit of analysis. Tasks, of course, require skill and knowledge to perform.

In this context, it is useful to delineate between hard and soft skills.

Hard skills can be thought of as the formulaic knowledge needed to perform a particular task, exemplified by STEM disciplines. High levels of numeracy, logical thinking, and the ability to retain information are key characteristics of the perfect student.

Given these idealised characteristics, it doesn't take much imagination to envision machines quickly surpassing human potential. Tireless and impartial software fuelled by unlimited data and computational power will increasingly outpace even the most gifted human practitioners.

On the other hand, soft skills are those that are innately human. Traits such as creativity, empathy, and the ability to influence others are likely to be far harder to reduce to formula. They are inherently protected by Polanyi's paradox. Put simply, Polanyi's paradox suggests that we *know more than we can tell*. In other words, we just inherently know how to do certain things – but often struggle to explain such knowledge to others. What makes someone a great storyteller, for example? Why can some people just put others at ease?

The subjective and ethereal nature of soft skills prevents them from being easily reduced to machine code.

That said, recent advances have certainly encroached. ChatGPT can now write a credible children's story, produce a passable poem in seconds, and even provide advice on how to negotiate the purchase of your next car. However, it is nascent and amateur at best. Soft skills take a lifetime to master.

Organisational Decision-Making

In the coming chapters, we will focus on an organisational task that seamlessly blends hard and soft skills: decision-making.

Decision-making is perhaps the most recurrent task in an organisation, pervasive throughout organisational layers, and a critical success factor. Good decisions create sustainable growth; bad decisions destroy shareholder value.

Most of us would consider ourselves to be effective, rational decision-makers. However, anyone who has spent any amount of time in a corporate environment knows that day-to-day decisions depart from rationality with alarming regularity.

Such is the frequency with which organisational leaders depart from rationality that one of the greatest challenges facing most organisations is how to overcome agency challenges. In other words, how do the owners of large organisations, i.e. the shareholders, protect themselves from the self-serving interests of the people appointed to run organisations on their behalf?

Corporate governance, the establishment of boards, and a myriad of incentive schemes have been established to redress this challenge to mixed effect. However, technology potentially offers a way of overcoming this obstacle by automating and augmenting human decisions while democratising data.

There is, however, something unique about human decision-making. The best human decision-makers can think in a non-linear manner. They can inspire followership and influence outcomes in a way that can result in transformative results for organisations. Steve Jobs would never have arrived at the iPod by thinking linearly about how to improve the Walkman. The iPhone would never have been envisioned by incrementally improving upon early mobile phones.

Deciding where to leverage technology to improve decisions and where to invest in human talent is highly complex. However, it is vitally important to consider.

In the following chapters, we will explore a model through which to frame this dilemma.

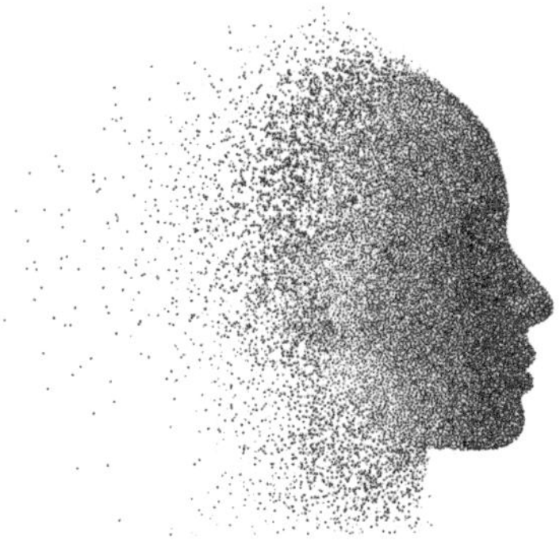

Chapter 2

A Model for Practice - Overview

"One machine can do the work of fifty ordinary men. No machine can do the work of one extraordinary man."

Elbert Hubbard

~ A Model For Practice Overview ~

My greatest hope for this book is that it helps to inform thinking and frame some well-established debates in a practical way. Technology should not be the sole domain of engineers; in fact, AI has brought technology closer to the average business leader than at any time in the past. As such, it is important to be curious, prepare, and act.

One of the things I have always found frustrating about nonfiction is being forced to read several hundred pages to understand the central themes. With ever-busier lives, many of us simply don't have the time or inclination to read a book cover to cover, which feels like a significant inhibitor to sharing knowledge.

With that in mind, I've set out a succinct summary of the proposed model and associated themes in the following chapter. Subsequent chapters explore each aspect of the model in greater detail, allowing you to choose how deep you want to go.

For those who skipped the introduction, and as a refresher for those who haven't, I will briefly recap the purpose of this book.

The world is changing rapidly on the back of advances in technology, and in particular, AI. Organisational leaders are facing a dizzying choice of technologies, many of which offer as much hyperbole as substance. Decision-making is one of the most recurrent activities in any organisation and a key success factor. Whilst technology has the potential to automate many day-to-day business decisions, human talent continues to have an important role to play. Thus, deciding where to leverage technology and where to double down on human talent is an existential dilemma for organisational leaders. Within this book, we will explore a model to support the beleaguered executive in navigating this minefield.

Framing the Debate

On a day-to-day basis, we make a dizzying number of decisions. Most of them are so trivial and familiar to us that they barely register as decisions at all.

If asked, most of us would likely suggest that we are highly rational in our choices. In fact, some have gone so far as to suggest that rational decision-making is one of the defining characteristics of our race. However, the truth is that, for the large part, we are anything but rational.

The concept of rational decision-making is derived from economics. To make an economically rational decision, a decision maker must consider all possible options, estimate the utility associated with each, and select that which has the highest probability of maximising a desired outcome. I paraphrase slightly, but you get the gist, and hopefully, the challenge is obvious. In a complex world where we are bombarded with information, time-constrained, and cognitively limited, it's simply not practical to make all our decisions in a strictly rational manner.

We live in a world where, for much of our evolution, making *timely* decisions has historically been more important than necessarily making *optimal* decisions. As decision makers we are bounded by both our cognitive ability and time. Consequently, Herbert Simon suggests that we *satisfice* in response to our *bounded rationality* – by making decisions that we consider to be *good enough.*[2]

We have evolved to shortcut decision-making processes by using heuristic cues and intuition. While we discuss this in more detail in Chapter 3, the key takeaway is that heuristics are rational decision-making processes, albeit shortcuts, while intuition can be thought of as *immediate understanding in the absence of reason.*[3]

Nobel-winning economist Daniel Kahneman, in his book, *Thinking, Fast and Slow*[4]*,* invites us to consider the guttural, instinctive basis for our decisions as originating from System 1 thinking. By contrast, more considered reasoning is associated with System 2. However, we are often unaware of which of these two systems is being called upon when making decisions. The inability to discern between these two different decision-making apparatuses can lead to a range of unintended *biases* and *systematic errors*.

---

2 SIMON, H. A. 1948. Administrative Behavior: A Study of the Decision-making Process in Administrative Organization, Macmillan.

3 EVANS, J. S. B. T. 2010. Intuition and reasoning: A dual-process perspective. *Psychological Inquiry,* 21, 313-326.

4 KAHNEMAN, D. A. 2011. *Thinking, Fast and Slow*, 1st ed. New York : Farrar, Straus and Giroux,

Let's now frame this within an organisational construct. Decision-making is one of the most recurrent activities in companies of any size. The larger the company, the more complex the decisions and associated decision-making processes. In small, owner-led firms, decision-making is relatively straightforward, with the owners making all material decisions themselves. As companies grow and ownership and management become separated, the process becomes far more complex.

Most would agree that organisations should be run to maximise the benefits for their owners. However, at scale, shareholders are dependent on the management teams appointed to run the organisation on their behalf. Due to information asymmetry and time constraints, shareholders have traditionally had limited option but to trust their appointees. The challenge, of course, is that conflict potentially arises between the interests of the shareholders and the interests of the management teams. In academic parlance, this is referred to as *agency conflict.*

As a shareholder, when someone within an organisation is making a financial decision on your behalf, you may reasonably expect that such decisions are optimal rather than satisfactory. Now, overlay the fact that human decision-makers are frail, cognitively limited, and time-constrained. That is a significant compromise versus the idealised state.

Historically, these challenges have been acknowledged and mitigated. Corporate governance, overseen by independent boards, and a myriad of incentive schemes have been devised to align interests and to ensure material decisions are made in a structured manner. A less-than-perfect system that has had to suffice in the absence of any viable alternative.

The situation is starting to change.

Machines, powered by intelligent automation and AI, increasingly provide alternatives to human decision-making. Fintech organisations, for example, now utilise machines to assess credit applications, making timely, rational, and highly repeatable decisions in seconds. Recruiters deploy software to review candidate CVs, eliminate bias, and create shortlists of candidates. In short, decision-making technology is transforming countless industries and functions.

In parallel, technology is reducing information asymmetry by providing greater actionable insight than at any point in the past. Shareholders and boards now potentially have more unfiltered information available to them than at any point in corporate history. This includes information related to high-stakes decisions such as acquisitions and divestments.

The reality, however, is that whilst tireless and impartial machines are well equipped to augment and support certain organisational [illegible] here are limits. Human judgement and experience [illegible] hly prized by organisations. When it comes to high stakes [illegible] data helps to inform the process, but it is not sufficient to [illegible] inal determination.

[illegible] world increasingly reduced to bits and bytes, the trend to [illegible] decisions is likely to continue at pace. That said, a balance [illegible] struck between human talent and machines.

As ever, there will be few absolutes, but the framework we will now explore helps leaders strike such a balance in a measured and considered manner.

A graphic of the framework follows on the next page.

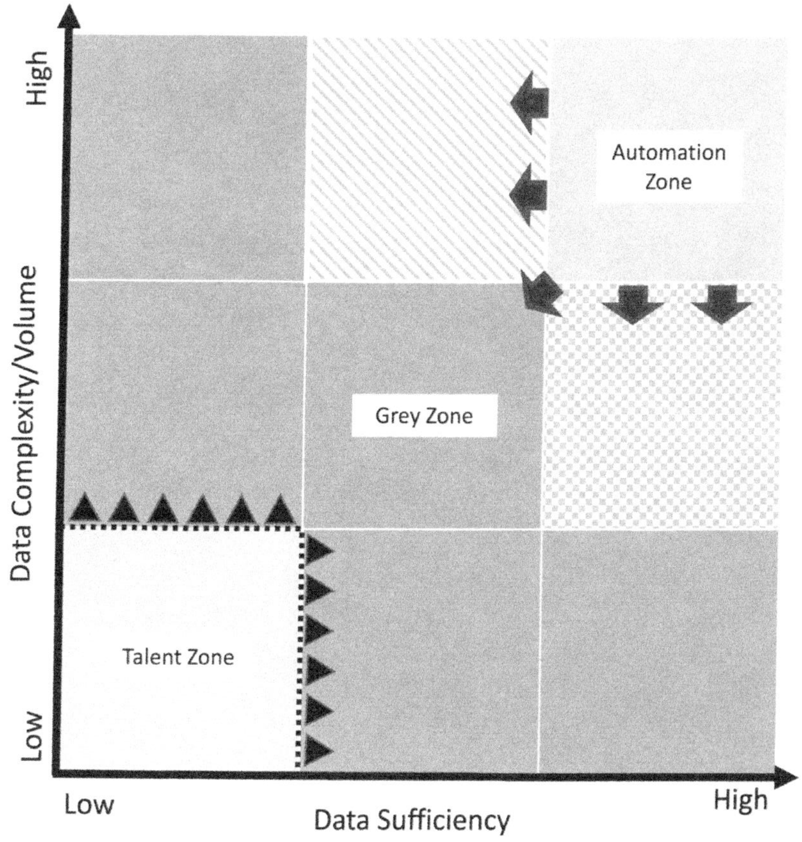

Key

- Accommodation & Resistance
- Connected Devices, Digital Operations, Synthetic Data & Machine Learning
- Connected Devices. Synthetic Data & Digital Operations Enables
- Machine Learning Enables

Definitions

- **Data Complexity/Volume:** the amount of data and associated complexity - available to inform a given decision.
- **Data Sufficiency:** the extent to which data alone is deemed sufficient to inform a given decision.

I would be surprised if the model on the opposite page made immediate sense at first glance, but we will explore each element in summary form below. These themes are then expanded upon in the chapters that follow.

Data Volume & Complexity

Data fuels automation. Although this statement has become a truism for most people, it's important to understand and digest.

Since ChatGPT first burst onto the scene in November 2022, AI has gripped the popular imagination. Foundational models such as ChatGPT are trained on unimaginable volumes of data. For example, Google's LLM, Gemini Ultra, was reported to have cost $191m in compute alone to train.[5] Offering these tools seemingly for free was a brilliant way of refining algorithms and generating yet more data. Millions of people have both wittingly and unwittingly provided further fuel to power these leviathans.

It may, however, come as a surprise to learn that we are at risk of running out of data. While we are generating more data now than at any time in history, a report by Stanford University suggests that we will run out of high-quality language data to train AI on by the end of 2024. Audio and visual files will be exhausted by the late 2030s.[6] Real-world data will increasingly be augmented by *synthetic data*, in other words, data created by machines for machines.

5 Artificial Intelligence Index Report 2024. AI Index Report 2024 – Artificial Intelligence Index.

6 Artificial Intelligence Index Report 2024. AI Index Report 2024 – Artificial Intelligence Index.

Regardless of the source, data serves as a catalyst for automation. The more data we have and the more complex it becomes, the more likely we are to require machine intelligence to make sense of it. Humans are pretty good at managing structured data but struggle with huge volumes of semi-structured and unstructured data. We are simply not designed to systematically process data at the kind of volume and complexity required by modern organisations.

So, *data volume and complexity* form the first axis of our model.

Data Sufficiency

As most organisational leaders recognise, raw data has limited value. What we need is *actionable insight*. In other words, we need data that helps to inform our decisions in meaningful ways. We refer to this principle as *data sufficiency* - the extent to which data is sufficient to inform a given decision.

Personal credit decisions serve as excellent examples of where rational, repeatable choices can be based on data. An applicant will have an income of X and expenses of Y. In many cases, it is a formulaic decision. The more information we have about an individual's spending habits and earnings, the better our decision will be. Fundamentally, it involves relatively simple math.

At the other extreme, few of us would consider data alone to be sufficient to determine whether we bought a particular company or hired a certain individual. In such instances, subjective criteria come into play based on human judgement and experience. A candidate may look brilliant on paper, but something may not click when you eventually meet in person.

So, *data sufficiency* forms the second axis of our model.

Automation Zone: Machines as Coping Pioneers

Where both data volume/complexity and sufficiency are high, machines potentially serve as *coping pioneers*.

In this decision zone, machines are capable of making highly repeatable, rational decisions at a rate that would be difficult for human agents to replicate. In such environments, machines are the only commercially sustainable way of coping with scale.

Deploying technology becomes a competitive advantage for an early adopter and a necessity if following the competition's lead. In this decision zone, machines displace and largely substitute for human labour. High-frequency trading platforms are a good example. Such platforms can analyse market data and make decisions that would be beyond the ability of any human agent to support. The industry simply would not exist without machine intelligence capable of making decisions in nanoseconds and executing trades in near real-time.

However, not only do machines enable organisations to *cope* efficiently with scale, but they also help to *pioneer* insight. Machines, powered by machine learning, can make sense of and discern patterns from complex semi-structured and unstructured data sets. This enables new opportunities to be identified by exploring patterns and connections that would otherwise be missed.

The collaboration between Google's DeepMind and Moorfields Eye Hospital, for example, derived unexpected insight into the early detection of systemic diseases. The project unexpectedly resulted in a non-invasive screening method that would have remained undiscovered had it not been for AI's ability to work across huge data sets and detect insight beyond the ability of even the most gifted medical professionals.

It is critical that organisations exploit technology within this decision zone. That said, there are challenges associated with doing so.

While we explore these issues further in Chapters 8 and 12, it is important to emphasise that strong governance is essential to protect organisations from unintended consequences. The training of machines, the sourcing of data, the transparency of the algorithms used for recommendations, and the degree of adaptive autonomy over time are critical concerns. Black box technology and machine learning can diminish transparency and heighten risks in these areas. Interestingly, however, there is increasing evidence that certain black box models outperform their more transparent counterparts.[7]

While these challenges are not insurmountable and should not be viewed as non-negotiable, they do deserve serious consideration and require active management.

Talent Zone: Engineering Bottlenecks

By contrast, where both data volume/complexity and data sufficiency are low, we encounter *engineering bottlenecks*.[8] In such instances, elite human talent differentiates organisational capability, with

7 Artificial Intelligence Index Report 2024. AI Index Report 2024 – Artificial Intelligence Index.

8 Term first coined by FREY, 2017, The future of employment: how susceptible are jobs to computerisation?

judgement and experience being highly prized.

The highest stake decisions made by organisations concern where to deploy scarce capital. In other words, where do we invest, and which acquisition targets should we consider?

In 2006, Disney's CEO, Bob Iger's proposed acquisition of Pixar met with fierce resistance from both the board and his advisors. Rationally, the numbers didn't stack up. $7.4 billion for a company with c.800 employees seemed a heroic gamble for the struggling organisation. Yet Iger saw subjective qualities in the organisation, including 'the level of talent and creative ambition, the commitment to quality, the storytelling ingenuity, the technology, the leadership structure, and the air of enthusiastic collaboration.'[9] Not only could Iger *creatively project* the future of animation and Pixar's transformational impact on Disney's ailing fortunes, but through sheer force of personality was able to bring everyone on board to make it happen. The rest, as they say, is history.

The ability to *creatively project the future* and *influence* others are uniquely human traits. Consider Christensen's, The Innovators Dilemma. Fundamentally, those who make linear progress are destined to be supplanted by those who can make conceptual leaps in thinking and leverage technical innovation.

It is precisely because these soft traits are subjective that makes them so hard to replicate, creating a unique source of competitive advantage. The human mind is perhaps the ultimate black box.

---

9 IGER, R. 2019. *The Ride Of A Lifetime*, Penguin Random House.

In this decision zone, leaders need to double down on human talent.

However, we must add a cautionary note. Soft decision criteria are hard to articulate rationally. Data asymmetry between the board and senior leadership will limit the formers ability to fully validate the basis for decisions and calls for significant degrees of trust. Decisions in this space are notoriously challenging. Despite potentially transformative impacts, corporate history is littered with examples of abject failure, and the reality remains that at least a third of acquisitions and mergers fail to realise their expected benefit.

Grey Zone

The Grey Zone lies between our two extremes, where the volume, complexity, and sufficiency of data are modest.

Both metaphorically and literally, the Grey Zone currently dominates our model. It is a space where neither humans nor machines are perfectly suited to decision-making and should be approached with care.

Take the example of a typical business case. It should be relatively easy to review the relative return on investment, net present value, and payback period across, say, five different projects. A strong argument for using impartial machine intelligence. However, the quality of the inputs and context must be carefully considered. Reading the room and understanding the subtleties that have gone into the projections of each is a matter best reserved for an experienced leader. The projections used within the model are likely to be highly subjective and tainted by bias. Thus, while a machine may be able to augment a decision with data and run the background math, human judgement will continue to play an important role in making a final decision.

The Grey Zone tends to be dominated by a myriad of narrow use cases, which can result in pilot paralysis. One service provider I spoke to highlighted that a particular client had over 1,200 active use cases!

While the investments in this decision zone may be smaller than those at the extremes of our model, the returns are much less reliable. The interaction between humans and machines is notoriously challenging. Change management, education, and user attitudes will be as critical to success as the technology itself.

Organisations should avoid overly focusing on the Grey Zone. It will consume significant time and investment and detract from the more appropriate focus areas we have highlighted. Investments in the Grey Zone are unlikely to materially differentiate an organisation - they will however quickly burn through scarce cash and resource.

The situation, however, will continue to evolve at pace.

Connected Devices

Although the Grey Zone currently dominates our model, it may not do so for long. Technology continues to advance exponentially.

Although it has fallen slightly out of vogue recently, a few years ago, everyone was talking about the Internet of Things (IoT). While it may be little more than a rebranding of existing technology, it remains a useful concept. IoT recognises a rapidly growing web of connected devices that translate the world into bits and bytes.

Although the parlance may have fallen out of regular use, the concept is still important.

The number of connected devices is rapidly increasing. From sensors that indicate when staff are in the office to the app on your phone that tracks how many steps you've taken today, it seems that almost everything is recording data in one form or another. Although these devices may serve subtly different purposes, they all share a common function: translating physical activity into machine-readable code.

Digital Operations

In parallel, organisations are no longer born out of bricks and mortar. Modern organisations are born digital - digitally native, if you will. Their operations and associated processes generate data from inception. With traditional companies scrambling to transform to remain relevant, the result is that, again, such organisations generate more data, or fuel, than at any point in the past.

Synthetic Data

As if the enormous amounts of data we are currently creating weren't sufficient, a new innovation promises to fill any remaining gaps. Where insufficient organic data exists to train machines, organisations are increasingly looking to use synthetic data to accelerate various use cases.

Synthetic data is data created by machines for machines. It can be produced quickly, at scale, and to exact standards - creating theoretically perfect training sets. This technology has the potential to eliminate bias by producing representative data samples that may not exist in the real world. While not without its challenges, synthetic data is an interesting option for organisations facing privacy and other commercial restrictions regarding their historical data.

Returning to our original axes, data will continue to grow exponentially. This influx of information will push use cases that historically resided in the Grey Zone to the furthest extremes of our model.

Machine Learning

As we highlighted previously, raw data alone is insufficient to power automation. Machine learning is increasingly critical in exploiting vast data sets and is progressing rapidly. LLMs are powered by complex machine learning algorithms, and whilst legislation is increasingly attempting to curb certain high-risk practices, the trend does not look set to abate. Machine learning will increasingly drive data sufficiency, increasing the scope for automating decisions that previously sat within the Grey Zone.

Accelerators Driving Tomorrow's Use Cases

The natural consequence of increasingly digital operations, the expanding numbers of connected devices, the evolution of synthetic data, and ever-more sophisticated machine learning is that machines will increasingly encroach on human domains. Leaders should constantly review their assumptions in light of these advances. If a particular use case has high potential but lacks data, what devices could be deployed to create the necessary fuel? Could synthetic data plug a gap? Where data exists but insight is limited, what machine learning techniques could be deployed to exploit it?

Again, considered choices must be made, but the most enlightened leaders will constantly look to the horizon rather than focusing on what's immediately in front of them today.

Accommodation & Resistance

Whilst connected devices, increasingly digital operations, synthetic data, and machine learning will see machines continue to encroach into human domains, multiple factors will keep their progress in check. The most obvious and hotly debated of these factors being legislation.

Legislation

There is fierce debate over the role of legislation in ensuring the responsible use of technology, particularly AI. On the one hand, pro-innovation advocates call for modest controls. On the other hand, proponents point to the existential risks associated with AI's impact and call for stringent guardrails to avoid dystopian futures. It is fair to say that legislators are divided at the time of writing.

The EU AI Act is the most comprehensive regulatory framework published to date governing the responsible use of AI. The EU has adopted a risk-based approach centred around prohibited systems, high-risk systems, and general-purpose AI. The legislation creates significant obligations on both suppliers and deployers of such technology, with emphasis on the latter.

That said, the legislation has been in the making since at least 2022. It is based on a phased introduction over 36 months and, by the commission's own admission, will be difficult to operationalise in the short term. However, it is stringent enough that Apple delayed deploying its latest AI-powered phone in Europe (this admittedly is speculation on my part).

Regardless of your philosophical perspective, legislation will play an increasingly important role in the coming years. It will both *accommodate and resist* the advance of technology. It will offer resistance by governing ethical deployment and will accommodate by enabling more conservative organisations to understand permissible boundaries and, in so doing, legitimise certain practices.

Regulators

For those operating in regulated industries, the attitudes of regulators are likely to continue to play a significant role in determining the responsible boundaries for technology. In the UK, for example, the recently released *pro-innovation approach to AI regulation*[10], devolves responsibility to the c.90 UK regulatory bodies for ensuring that its non-legislative framework is applied in practice. The approach is intended to ensure that measures are proportionate to the associated risks and domain-specific challenges. I rather suspect that this obfuscation will result in more confusion than benefit.

Regardless, regulators will play a significant role in ensuring that their charges do not overextend while maintaining transparency and explainability. We spoke to several leaders operating in heavily regulated sectors, all of whom highlighted the close working relationships they had with their regulatory counterparts. They also pointed out that in a rapidly evolving space, the relationship was a two-way learning process.

---

10 2023, A pro-innovation approach to AI regulation. https://www.gov.uk/government/publications/ai-regulation-a-pro-innovation-approach/white-paper

Customer Attitudes

In a like manner, customers will play a significant role in determining the future. Leaders recognise that dehumanised banking, medical practice, and expert advice will meet with resistance. That said, generational attitudes are shifting, with many of the more digitally savvy sections of society valuing ease of use and efficiency. As one financial services CTO observed, 'it would be a bold person who would dare bet against digitisation hitting a limit any time soon and there being any limits to each new generation's acceptance of greater digitisation and the services that they consume'. Consumer and customer attitudes should not, however, be overlooked, and certainly should not be taken for granted.

Professional Bodies

Finally, one of the last bastions of defence for certain traditional white-collar professions is likely to be professional bodies. In the US, for example, practising law without being a qualified lawyer is illegal, posing interesting challenges for providers looking to disrupt this space. In the UK, although practising law without the relevant qualifications is not illegal, non-lawyers do not benefit from legal privilege, which is essential for protecting clients' sensitive information. Similarly, accounting standards have become so opaque in recent years that they no longer align with common sense and increasingly require expert interpretation. As one senior leader commented, the consequence is that certain professions have become 'frozen in time'. With many solutions challenging these professions, it will be fascinating to see where accommodations are made.

A Look to the Future

The purpose of the foregoing model is not to offer absolutes. Nor is it intended to highlight the potential of GAI or any other specific form of technology. The intention is to help organisational leaders frame the debate between technology and talent and to do so in a future-proof manner. Whatever happens from here on in, the fundamental elements of the model will remain valid; the only question will be how many organisational decisions reside in each of our decision zones.

Leaders should focus on the future rather than just reacting to immediate challenges. They must anticipate what's coming next, with top executives laying the groundwork for tomorrow's success by investing in the right tools today. Unwittingly deploying legacy technology can harm shareholder value. Similarly, using technology, especially AI, merely to *check a box* is not a great strategy.

Leaders should look to the extremes of our model for the best returns.

The Grey Zone should be approached with care, despite being an area that most feel comfortable experimenting in. It will be increasingly disrupted by technology leveraging connected devices, digital operations, synthetic data, and machine learning. As a result, assumptions should be revisited regularly, and leaders should challenge themselves to think about how they accelerate high-potential use cases.

Technology alone will not define corporate success. While technology is easily replicated and creates a short-term competitive advantage, the human ability to creatively project the future and influence others is irreplicable. Its value in high-stakes decisions should not be overlooked in an increasingly technology-driven world.

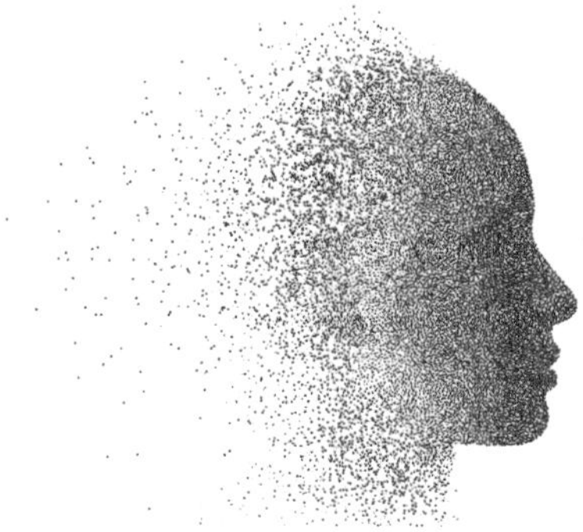

Chapter 3

Background:

Human Decision-Making

"Nothing is more difficult, and therefore more precious, than to be able to decide."

Napoleon Bonaparte

~ Human Decision-Making ~

History is littered with examples of celebrated personalities who have made critical decisions that have resulted in differentiated outcomes and altered the course of history - from Napoleon's ill-fated invasion of Russia in 1812 to Stanislav Petrov, who averted a nuclear war by ignoring the advice of his console in 1983. On a less grandiose scale, good judgement is highly prized in nearly all professions and serves to differentiate elite workers.

I've always been fascinated by choice. As a philosophy student, I was intrigued by the notion of free will. Without disappearing into an abstract monologue, I was equally intrigued by the fact that some people seem to make an endless succession of good choices while the less fortunate among us do the exact opposite.

As a graduate, I naively assumed that organisations filled with bright minds would make well-informed, rational decisions. Of course, the further I progressed in my career, the more it became apparent that organisational decision-making departs from rationality with alarming regularity. I would sit in meetings where the correct decision appeared obvious, and yet, for various reasons, a different choice was made.

As technology advanced and data-driven insights increased, I became intrigued by the potential impact of automation on decision-making. Whenever I looked at my pension portfolio, for example, I wondered why a machine wasn't picking stocks on my behalf. It seemed like a highly rational process where access to data and the ability to process the same in real-time were essential ingredients for success. In contrast, deciding what colour to paint my living room felt like a decision I was much better suited to make. As an aside, at the time of writing, I have just finished decorating my room for the third time in eighteen months, twelve of which I spent travelling!

It seemed obvious to me that there are choices best suited to machine intelligence. Intelligence defined by high IQ, unlimited computational ability, tireless processing capacity, and access to relevant and expansive data sets. Although the technology has only recently begun to emerge, it has always felt like a matter of time.

It was also clear that certain decisions benefit from human intelligence (my living room aside). We have a natural ability to abstract beyond data, take account of subjective information, use intuition, and assess the potential impact of our choices on others. These traits can make us highly effective decision-makers in the right circumstances.

Utility Theory – Laplacian Minds

As I began researching human decision-making, I stumbled across utility theory. Born out of traditional economics, utility theory depicts humans as perfectly rational agents who meticulously weigh options to maximise value. According to this doctrine, we should review all available choices, estimate associated probabilities, and calculate the expected utility of each choice to make the optimal decision. It's a neat and tidy model, but it's far removed from the reality of human cognition.[11]

Allais Paradox serves to demonstrate the point. Imagine being presented with the following choices:

- Option 1A: You will receive a guaranteed £1 million.
- Option 2A: You will be entered for a lottery with an 89% chance of winning £1 million, a 10% chance of winning £5 million, and a 1% chance of winning nothing.

When faced with these options, most people opt for the certainty of the guaranteed £1 million over the gamble. Even though the lottery offers excellent odds of walking away with the same or higher payout than Option 1A, the chance of losing a guaranteed £1 million is too great a risk for many.

Now consider a second set of choices:

- Option 1B: You will be entered into a lottery with an 11% chance of winning £1 million and an 89% chance of winning nothing.
- Option 2B: You will be entered into a lottery with a 10% chance of winning £5 million and a 90% chance of winning nothing.

In this scenario, the same individuals who opted for Option 1A and

11 FISHBURN, P. C. & KOCHENBERGER, G. A. 1979. TWO PIECE VON NEUMANN MORGENSTERN UTILITY FUNCTIONS. Decision Sciences, 10, 503-518.

the guaranteed £1 million often choose Option 2B. When offered this choice, many are willing to accept slightly worse odds for the possibility of a larger reward.

At first glance, the difference between the decisions in these scenarios may seem perfectly reasonable. However, if you explore the math, it reveals an inconsistency that challenges utility theory. It might be worth taking a moment to think this through.

A strictly rational decision-maker would make the same decision in both circumstances. The probabilities between the two options are the same.

Yet, the shift from risk aversion in the first scenario to risk-seeking behaviour in the second exposes a flaw in human decision-making. This phenomenon is known as the certainty effect. In the second set of options, where there is no guaranteed outcome, we are more inclined to take risks for the chance of a greater payoff.

When I first read this in *Thinking, Fast and Slow*, I was intrigued. At the time, I ran procurement for a FTSE100 company. I wondered what my team of highly rational commercial professionals would make of the paradox. I sent the options to each of them, and they voted accordingly. As predicted by the paradox, at least half of them made different choices in each of the two scenarios.

Utility theory imagines a "Laplacian Demon."[12] I love this expression! It arguably requires a mind equipped with infinite knowledge,

12 GIGERENZER, G. & GOLDSTEIN, D. G. 1996. Reasoning the fast and frugal way: Models of bounded rationality. Psychological Review, 103, 650-669.

unlimited time, and God-like cognitive ability. However, the reality for most of us is very different. At the time, I was somewhat perplexed. My illusion of human rationality had been shattered!

Bounded Rationality & Real-World Human Decision-Making

Herbert Simon introduced the concept of "bounded rationality"[13] to describe the gap between idealised rationality and actual human behaviour. He observed that we are bound by our cognitive ability, our temporal limitations, and our access to information. When faced with real-world complexity, we *satisfice* rather than optimise. In other words, we make decisions that are simply *good enough*.

Without effective coping mechanisms, we would quickly become paralysed in the face of real-world complexity. Heuristics, for example, are simple mental shortcuts that help us simplify choices and play a material part in day-to-day decisions. These efficient cognitive processes allow us to make judgements quickly and with minimal effort, focusing on the most relevant information and cheerfully discarding the rest.

Imagine trying to choose a restaurant in a new city. You might spend the evening in the establishment with the longest queue, assuming it's popular for a reason. Or you might opt for a chain that you recognise. These mental shortcuts save time and energy. There are a countless number of heuristics that we call upon in day-to-day life.

To delve slightly deeper into how we make decisions, we can turn

13 SIMON, H. A. 1948. Administrative Behavior: A Study of the Decision-making Process in Administrative Organization, Macmillan.

to the work of psychologist Daniel Kahneman, a Nobel laureate renowned for his research on judgement and decision-making. In *Thinking, Fast and Slow*, Kahneman introduces the idea of two systems that drive the way we think:

1. System 1: A fast, automatic, and intuitive mode of thinking. It describes the mental processes that help us make rapid decisions with minimal effort - like recognising a brand on the high street or sensing danger.

2. System 2: A slow, deliberate, and analytical mode of thinking. It kicks in when we engage in careful reasoning, or when we deliberate between choices - like deciding which mortgage to select.

Kahneman argues that while System 1 is essential for navigating daily life efficiently, it is also prone to systematic errors and biases. System 2 has the capacity to override these mistakes, but requires time, energy and attention, which we can't always spare.

Our reliance on System 1 means that intuition plays a significant role in our decision-making process. Intuition can be thought of as immediate comprehension in the absence of reason.[14] It's the gut feeling that tells you something is wrong during a negotiation or that a particular person is the right individual to solve your talent crisis, even though you've barely done more than shake their hand. Intuitive decisions are made without conscious reasoning, drawing on patterns we've recognised subconsciously over time.

---

14 EVANS, J. S. B. T. 2010. Intuition and reasoning: A dual-process perspective. Psychological Inquiry, 21, 313-326.

However, intuition isn't infallible. Our intuitive judgements can be influenced by cognitive biases - systematic errors in thinking that can distort our perceptions and lead to flawed decisions. These biases are inherent in System 1 thinking and can affect even the most experienced professionals.

For example, the way that information is relayed to us can significantly impact our decisions. When someone we trust presents two options, framing one with enthusiasm and purpose and the second as an afterthought, it immediately biases our judgement. In a like manner, the so-called framing effect highlights how people react differently to choices depending on whether they are framed in terms of potential gains or losses, even if the outcomes are equivalent. We saw this in action with the previous example of Allais Paradox. I could go on, but I suspect that few people need convincing of the propensity for bias in day-to-day judgements.

Traditional economic theories often portray decision-making as a purely logical, cold, cognitive process. However, emotion, and in particular, regret, play a significant role in real-world decision-making. Regret, in this context, is the painful realisation that the current situation compares unfavourably with what might have otherwise been.[15]

We experience regret most acutely when decisions are complex, when options are closely matched in value, when probabilities are murky, or when we're forced to make trade-offs between two important factors, such as work and family. The more significant

15 SUGDEN, R. 1985. Regret, recrimination and rationality. *Theory and Decision*, 19, 77-99.

and uncertain the decision, the greater the potential for regret.

My mother would likely retort to what I've just written by highlighting that there's no point in crying over spilt milk. This is, of course, true. Regret after the event is somewhat futile. However, while regret is experienced after a decision is made, its *anticipation* plays a profound role at the point of choice.

Our natural aversion to regret means we often subconsciously factor the possibility of future regret into our current decisions. Depending on the context and our natural bias, this can lead us to make either risk-averse or risk-seeking choices. For instance, we might avoid a risky investment to prevent a potential loss, or we might take a bold leap to avoid regretting a missed opportunity. Academics label this phenomenon as the *minimax regret principle*.[16]

Regret serves a valuable purpose. It enables us to learn from our experiences and adjust our future decisions accordingly. It's a feedback mechanism that encourages us to course-correct actions that haven't served us well and adopt more considered approaches moving forward. Ignoring regret would mean dismissing an essential aspect of our decision-making apparatus.

Hopefully, by now, it is apparent that most of us cannot consistently make wholly rational decisions - certainly not against traditional economic definitions. Yet there is something very compelling about human judgement. History is littered with people who have made outstanding decisions.

---

16 ZEELENBERG, M. 1999. Anticipated regret, expected feedback and behavioral decision making. Journal of Behavioral Decision Making, 12, 93-106.

On September 26, 1983, at the height of the Cold War, Stanislav Petrov, a lieutenant colonel in the Soviet Air Defence Forces, played a pivotal role in averting a potential nuclear catastrophe. While on duty at the Serpukhov-15 bunker near Moscow, Petrov's console suggested that a missile had been launched from the US towards the Soviet Union. Such were the tensions between the two nations that military procedure dictated an immediate retaliative strike. Initially, however, Petrov rationalised that there must be an error; the US would not launch a single missile. However, over the course of the next few minutes, his systems reported a growing number of missiles headed in the Soviet direction. Petrov's instinct, however, was that the system was malfunctioning, and he reported the incident as a false alarm. Despite ignoring direct military protocol, his actions undoubtedly averted a full-scale nuclear strike that would have changed the course of history.

By way of further example, Alan Mulally took over as CEO of Ford.[17] The company had been struggling for years and faced bankruptcy. Mulally immediately took out a $23.6 billion loan, mortgaging Ford's assets as collateral. His 'One Ford' plan involved using the secured funds to improve the balance sheet, restructure the organisation, and invest in new products. A bold and decisive move that faced staunch criticism internally and externally.

In 2008, the US economy reeled as the bottom fell out of the subprime mortgage market. The motor industry was hit hard, with people tightening their belts and avoiding large capital outlays. In response

17 EDMONSON, A. & JUNG, O. 2021. The Turnaround at Ford Motor Company. Harvard Business School.

Mulally was to demonstrate his unique leadership and decision-making qualities to the pending bankruptcy of two of Ford's largest competitors, Chrysler and General Motors. Reasoning that their demise would have significant negative consequences on Ford's own supply chain, he testified on their behalf in front of Congress. Ford's own superior liquidity, afforded by the loan facilitated by Mulally, allowed it to avoid a government bailout and continue to invest in the company's future throughout the financial crisis. Again, the rest is history.

We could explore innumerable examples of outstanding intuitive human decision-making, but what would likely underpin the majority of them is bold, creative, and almost unfathomable decisions that, at the time, attracted as much opposition as support.

Part of the challenge in understanding human decision-making is that the human mind is a complex backbox system. As Kahneman highlights, many of us do not understand our own mind when making a decision, so what chance do we have of explaining the basis of our more creative decisions to someone else?

Gut feeling, instinct, and intuition are murky concepts that powerfully influence decisions. However, their subjectivity makes them prone to error and bias. Without a full understanding of where our confidence arises, it is all too easy for that confidence to be fundamentally flawed.

Countless books have been written on human decision-making, transcending disciplines from philosophy to economics. Doing justice to the subject here is challenging. Suffice, however, to highlight that human decision-making involves few absolutes; we all make decisions differently, and our judgement, experience, and intuition make each of us unique.

What is clear, however, is that most of us do not make consistent rational decisions. Our reliance on System 1 thinking, our anticipation of regret, our cognitive limitations, and the scarcity of time all lead us to satisfice rather than optimise. Yet, for all of its potential frailty, history would look very different if the likes of Mulally, Petrov, and countless others had not backed their distinctly human basis for decisions.

For most of history, the foregoing debate has been interesting but largely theoretical. Why spend time debating the merits of human decision-making in the absence of alternatives? However, the situation is changing rapidly with the emergence of increasingly smart automation. For the first time machines potentially offer a credible alternative to human cognitive frailty, and it is to that subject that we now turn.

Key Takeaways

- Very few human decision-makers make consistently rational decisions owing to cognitive limitations, lack of time, and imperfect information
- Human decision-making is made using a combination of heuristics and intuition, often without conscious distinction between the two, making it subject to bias and error
- Bounded rationality results in decision-makers satisficing rather than optimising, in other words making decisions which are merely good enough
- The human mind is perhaps the ultimate black box

- Human decision-making, despite its apparent frailty, can result in transformative outcomes

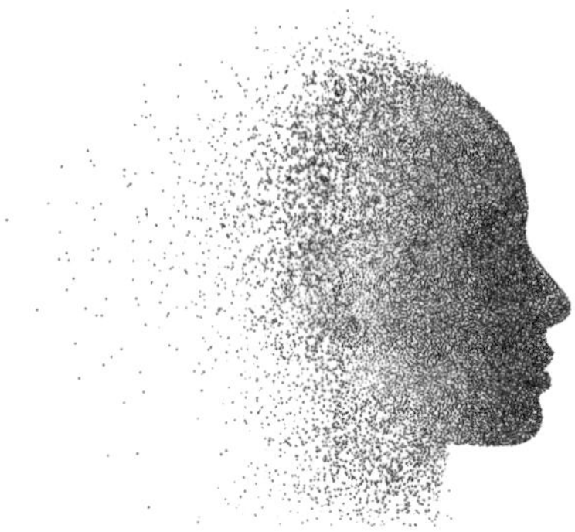

Chapter 4

Background:

Machine Decision-Making

"If a machine is expected to be infallible, it cannot also be intelligent."

Alan Turing

~ Machine Decision-Making ~

Recent advances in technology have very definitely blurred the lines between human and machine domains. Back in 1996, I remember sitting in philosophy lectures and being introduced for the first time to the Turing Test. The test was presented as an abstract thought experiment intended to determine whether a machine was capable of exhibiting human-like intelligence. The theoretical idea involved an independent moderator posing questions in natural language text to both a human and a machine. The machine was considered to have passed the test if the independent moderator was unable to distinguish between the two responses. Not in terms of correctness but in terms of whether the response had organic or inorganic origination. It captured my imagination.

I have watched with interest in the nearly thirty years since then as computers have moved through increasingly impressive feats. It was only in 1997 that IBM's Deep Blue first defeated Garry Kasparov over the course of a six-game match. It took a further 14 years before, in 2011, IBM's Watson mastered Jeopardy, beating former champions Ken Jennings and Brad Rutter. I remember being impressed that Watson had seemingly mastered human language processing, but I couldn't help but wonder what IBM's shareholders thought about its multi-million-dollar investment in Watson's AI capability!

In 2016 Google's AlphaGo defeated Lee Sedol at the ancient board game, Go. The game is played on a 19x19 board, each of which can have a number of different states. Without getting into the intricacies of the rules, it has been estimated that there are approximately 2.1×10^{170} legal positions. To put this number in context, there are more potential moves in a single game of Go than there are atoms in the observable universe. Mastery of Go takes a lifetime and is considered by many to be the pinnacle of strategy, calling for a heady mix of memory, premeditation, and creativity. The victory by AlphaGo was heralded as a major advance in deep learning and neural networks.

Of course, broader automation has advanced at a rapid pace in parallel. At the same time as machines were mastering chess, Jeopardy, and Go, industry was being transformed by the so-called fourth industrial revolution.

On the high street, we were introduced to self-service checkouts in supermarkets, semiautonomous vehicles were introduced onto our roads, industrial robots were introduced to automate manual tasks, and robotic surgical procedures began to make minimally invasive procedures a reality. Whilst they may be great for gaming, machines, it appeared, were also pretty good at performing a range of tasks historically considered the domain of human agents!

I became intrigued by what had changed to enable the sudden and rapid acceleration of technology. It was tempting to simply point to Moore's Law to explain the progress. Perhaps compute was now simply more powerful and accessible. Perhaps this additional compute combined with linear research into neural networks, and other sophisticated programming techniques was finally yielding long-anticipated results. I wasn't convinced, though.

An Epistemological Defence

As I began conducting my own research, I came across what many would likely consider a reasonably abstract text. The book was entitled 'What Computers Still Can't Do' and written by a technology philosopher named Hubert Dreyfus. It was published in 1972 when technology, and in particular AI, was still relatively nascent.

Despite my many years in industry, I've always been drawn to philosophers. The abstraction and purity of their thought processes can be enlightening. While engineers typically ask whether we *can* do something, philosophers are far more likely to question whether we *should*. They tend to look past the immediacy of the present to consider questions in the abstract.

In any event, the text I discovered set out an *epistemological* defence against machines. I include that word deliberately because I think it's a great one to master and drop casually into conversations! Epistemology concerns the nature, scope, and limitations of knowledge.

In this instance, Dreyfus had examined the nature of machine intelligence and believed that it was about to reach its limit. As a reader, I could sense Dreyfus' confidence that his treatise would stand the test of time, which piqued my interest.

Dreyfus highlighted that for machines to ever approximate human intelligence and decision-making, they would need to be able to distinguish the essential from the non-essential, use cues that remain on the fringe of consciousness, and, perhaps my favourite, "situate the individual with respect to a paradigm case".[18] I'm still not entirely sure I understand what that last statement means, but it is a beautiful turn of phrase.

The essence of Dreyfus's argument is simply that humans are perfectly adapted to complex, real-world environments precisely because they are situated within them. Philosophers are never shy of stating the obvious, and in this instance, Dreyfus points to our decision-making mastery as a consequence of "being in the world". In any given situation, we typically have immediate and full comprehension of our surroundings.

Imagine being blindfolded and moved to a new location. Even before the blindfold were removed, you would have a strong sense of what was happening around you. The physicality of your handling, the distance covered, the terrain, the nature and tone of the voices around you, and the circumstances leading up to your current predicament would all be strong cues. You would absorb and interpret all of this information subconsciously and in real-time.

As the blindfold was removed, you would likely already be braced for what was to follow. With kind hands, laughing voices, gentle handling, and a date proximal to your birthday, you would likely be expecting to come face to face with a birthday cake or a crowd of people shouting surprise. Having been apprehended whilst coming home late at night, you would be braced for something more sinister.

18 DREYFUS, H. L. 1972. What computers still can't do : a critique of artificial reason

Regardless of the situation, as the blindfold was removed, you would quickly take in your surroundings and start processing information. From that point forward, your decisions would be based on your immediate comprehension of your surroundings and the broader context.

Dreyfus invites us to imagine a machine performing a similar cognitive exercise. For machines to match human performance, Dreyfus argues, there is an assumption that "all knowledge can be formalised, that is, that whatever can be understood can be expressed in terms of logical relations, more exactly in terms of Boolean functions".[19] In other words, every element of the relatively simple experience we have just recounted would need to be reduced to bits and bytes. Even if such a thing were possible, the context would only have to change slightly to render a machine powerless to respond.

Dreyfus also suggests that machines deal with facts, which have traditionally been relayed to them by human engineers. Human agents, by contrast, continually learn based on experience, going through what he describes as *conceptual revolutions*. As we mature, we reach a point where few fixed responses are left, and we experience a life of adaptiveness based on situation, context, and lived experience.

Expert Systems

For many of the years that followed the publication of this work, Dreyfus's defence held firm. Until relatively recently, most intelligent systems fell within the definition of what we might refer

19 DREYFUS, H. L. 1972. What computers still can't do : a critique of artificial reason

to as expert systems. While definitions vary, common amongst them is the notion of an automated system that substitutes for, or in some instances, augments the performance of a role historically performed by a human expert.

The most common forms of expert systems are rule-based, well suited to structured data and narrow use cases and calling for largely predetermined responses. It is worth reflecting on the fact that computers originated in laboratories before moving to server rooms and gradually more broadly into the public domain. The challenge for rule-based systems, as heralded by Dreyfus, is that the world is complex, and reducing even narrow use cases to code is time-consuming and expensive.

I remember working at a large educational organisation that had partnered with a leading technology company to create a digital mentor using an early form of AI. The idea was relatively simple. Take a given textbook, digitise the content, and overlay a virtual tutor to help guide the students as they mastered the subject. I remember thinking it was a great idea. Imagine reading a text and being able to ask questions of an intelligent mentor when you began to struggle.

We had thousands of titles as a company, and I could intuitively understand the appeal of the product we were collaborating to build. It was perhaps not quite bleeding-edge, but it was at the forefront of the transformation of traditional education.

After several months I saw an early demonstration of the resultant tool. It was disappointing, to say the least. It had largely been designed to respond to set questions, providing predetermined responses. There was no dynamism, and it would take an inordinate amount of time to build out a workable version for a single textbook, let alone the entire back catalogue.

The use case sounds narrow, but the reality is that each book would require a bespoke set of expertly engineered replies, and because of the nature of learning, the questions posed by students were too numerous to encapsulate through fixed responses.

The project was eventually abandoned. Given recent advances in Generative AI, the example may seem somewhat antiquated, but it was, in fact, only 7 years ago and was backed at the time by two multi-billion-dollar organisations.

Compute has undoubtedly become cheaper and more accessible. Public cloud has enabled would-be developers to spin up environments quickly and cheaply, whilst no-code software suites have enabled the acceleration of minimal viable products. However, the single biggest accelerator is the fact that machines have left server rooms and are now very much in the real world.

Digital Worlds

Dreyfus was quite right. Mainframes and servers sitting in laboratories would always struggle to deal with real-world complexity. However, the world has become far more digitally connected in the 50-odd years since his publication.

By the time I had left the safety of university, mobile phones had become far more ubiquitous, while laptops became increasingly commoditised. The internet was burgeoning, and music had become increasingly digital. Two things were beginning to happen. Machines were being deployed far more broadly than at any time in the past, and consequently, more and more data about our world was being reduced to machine-readable code.

Fast-forward a few years, and smartphones have transformed the way that we think about mobile computing. Devices capable of sending basic messages, facilitating voice calls, and, if you were lucky, playing rudimentary games had been transformed into technological Swiss Army Knives. Devices like Alexa became popular to support a range of basic household tasks, while in industry, organisations began to increasingly digitise operations. We began to talk about digital natives, organisations born in a digital age and unencumbered by bricks, mortar, and legacy debt.

By any definition, machines were now in the world and increasingly translating it into bits and bytes.

I recently bought my first electric vehicle. One of the things I'm fascinated about is the fact that it is basically a mobile sensor. The 360-degree cameras translate the world in real-time into machine-readable code, enabling the car to do a host of clever things. It can come and find me in the car park whilst avoiding obstacles, automatically adjust my speed on the motorway to take account of the idiot in front of me, and prevent me from inadvertently crossing the intersection when I've lost concentration (protecting me from the idiot behind the wheel). Whether you like the concept of electric vehicles or not, they are amazing pieces of kit. They also produce an amazing amount of information about the real world that they are able to act upon.

Moral Machines

Sticking with this theme for a second, let's consider machine decision-making in this context. Machines are, at least in theory, capable of tirelessly processing information with perfect rationality. Depending on the amount of compute, they can do so in close to real-time.

Consequently, we cannot be far away from accepting that EVs may be better drivers than the average human. Once we get to that juncture the world gets a little bit crazy. Firstly, I suspect cars will increasingly cease looking like electric horse-drawn carriages, and a more functional shape will emerge. I've always liked the notion of a spherical vehicle that can turn in 360 degrees and absorb impact equally from any direction. I digress. The most significant change will be that EVs will soon be able to determine how to distribute harm.

In an unavoidable, high-speed collision scenario, human beings merely react. If we are travelling at high speed and faced with a choice of swerving one way and hitting person X or swerving the other way and hitting person Y, it is likely to be a lottery. A whole bunch of subconscious mental and physical variables will play into the outcome. I suspect few people would suggest that they did anything other than simply act in the moment and that a decision was not made on any kind of conscious level.

Machines will be different.

Imagine the same scenario. A connected machine may have enough information to determine who person X and person Y actually are.

Person X turns out to be Mr Andrew Hall, a 93-year-old single man. Andrew is a widow, father, beloved grandfather, has not worked for 30 years, and lives off a state pension. Person Y is Mrs Yvonne Sing, a wife, mother of three, and a neurosurgeon employed by Great Ormond Street Hospital. The decision-making systems of the car will have made such determination in real-time. Which way should the EV swerve?

It's a tough call, but I suspect that most of us would lean the same way.

Thirty years ago, I would have considered this an abstract thought experiment. Sitting here now, it is the very near future.

A fantastic article called The Moral Machine Experiment covers this topic in detail.[20] It's a great read. The synopsis is that the authors conduct quantitative research into the type of scenario outlined above and based on over 40 million votes from more than 233 countries, ranked different types of human beings based on their perceived value to society. Spoiler alert: the lowest ranked is criminal, and the highest ranked is a female doctor. In actual fact, they playfully mixed up the list and included two animals. The lowest ranked is a cat, criminal ranks just above our feline friends, whilst the ever-faithful dog trumps the felon!

In a world where we strive to create equality, promote diversity, and scorn prejudice, this may make unsettling reading. However, it is a fact. We are not all equal in the eyes of an algorithm. Such algorithms

---

20 AWAD, E., DSOUZA, S., KIM, R., SCHULZ, J., HENRICH, J., SHARIFF, A., BONNEFON, J.-F. & RAHWAN, I. 2018. The Moral Machine experiment. Nature, 563, 59-64.

will soon decide our relative merits, and whilst this example is extreme, it hopefully serves to make a point. It also highlights why legislation is needed to ensure that basic human rights are preserved.

Personally, I've always been a utilitarian. I subscribe to the simple doctrine that societal decisions should be made on the basis of maximising outcomes for the majority. I equally understand that many people have far more deontological belief systems (again, another great word to master and drop obnoxiously into conversation). Deontological belief systems are defined by those who believe that certain acts are never permissible. Some would argue, for example, that killing another human is never acceptable, regardless of the circumstances.

A utilitarian would likely accept that killing 5 people to save one million would make sense. A deontologist would likely disagree. The difference between the two positions is extreme.

However, the important question for our purposes is what ethical framework should be used to frame machine decision-making. In the days of our good friend Dreyfus, these questions were largely moot. But with the explosion of data and machines increasingly operating in the real world, they need to be considered far more urgently.

The Rise of AI

The advance of AI complicates matters further. Expert systems were never likely to trouble ethical realms. In most instances, they were narrow in scope, programmed, and abstracted from the real world. AI is different.

One of the things that I've found somewhat bemusing in recent months is that everyone is talking about AI, but very few share a common understanding of what AI is. For many years, it has barely mattered. People have talked about *human-like intelligence* without really needing to probe what that means in practice. When you consider it, to talk about human-like intelligence doesn't really mean a great deal, given the wide variety of intelligence exhibited by our race.

Perhaps more useful is the definition offered within the recently published EU AI Act. While we explore this in greater detail in Chapter 12, suffice to highlight that the definition points to the ability of a system to *infer* decisions, recommendations, and outputs. The definition also refers to adaptiveness and autonomy.

AI solutions then, rather than being explicitly programmed, infer from inputs. They are able to act with autonomy and to adapt over time. Machine learning is inherent in this definition, although not expressly called out. So, to return to Dreyfus and his second epistemological defence, machines can increasingly learn in much the same way as humans do. They are in context, as a result of sensors and connected devices, they can translate the world into bits and bytes, and they learn and adapt with autonomy.

In recent months, commentators have increasingly begun to discuss the notion of agentic AI. As ever, while there is much hyperbole, I suspect that few would be able to offer a compelling definition. It's tempting to recount Pickering's Mangle of Practice, another reasonably obscure text, where the author outlines a post-humanist definition of agency. It is worth a read for those interested in both sociology and technology. But for our purposes, it will suffice to highlight that the key principle of agency is, *intentionality*. Intentionality points to an agent's ability to work towards a goal or future state with both adaptability and autonomy. Until very recently, intentionality was limited to organic agents, but emergent technology has accorded ever greater agency to machines. In narrow contexts, agency should be carefully considered but carries modest risk; as technology becomes broader in application, agency becomes a far higher-risk development. We cover this in further detail in Chapter 12.

We've covered a mere 50 or so years in this chapter and neglected to mention quantum computing or Artificial General Intelligence. Yet, we've already gone from abstracted expert systems to autonomous, inference-based systems capable of demonstrating increasing degrees of agency that will be capable of distributing harm.

We can debate the magnitude and impact of technology, but tireless, impartial machines with access to almost unlimited cognitive capacity and data will undoubtedly play an important role in the near future.

We go on to explore this within an organisational context.

Key Takeaways

- Traditional AI has been dominated by expert systems which are expensive, laborious, and challenging to programme
- Historically machines have been abstracted from the world and reliant on expert knowledge to programme
- Connected devices increasingly translate the world into bits and bytes, whilst machine learning enables machines to

overcome traditional epistemological issues
- Machines are capable of processing information with tireless impartiality
- Black box technology needs to be considered with care

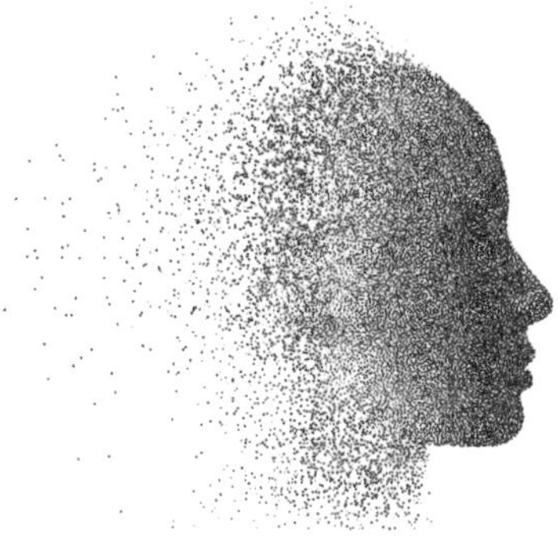

Chapter 5

Background:

Organisational Decision-Making

"Organizational effectiveness does not lie in that narrow-minded concept called rationality. It lies in the blend of clearheaded logic and powerful intuition."

Henry Mintzberg

~ Organisational Decision-Making ~

So far, we've taken a whistle-stop tour through human and machine decision-making. We've highlighted that human agents depart from rationality with alarming frequency, often fail to distinguish between System 1 and System 2 thinking, and are prone to making decisions that can lead to bias and systematic error. By contrast, machines can make highly repeatable rational decisions with tireless impartiality and increasingly translate the physical world into bits and bytes.

Organisations collide both machine and human decision making.

Decision-making is one of the most recurrent activities in any organisation. Complex decision processes underpin every staff appointment, every approved business case, and every acquisition. At lower levels in the organisation decisions determine which purchase orders are approved, which invoices are paid and when, and even what brand of coffee stocks our kitchens. Good decisions create shareholder wealth (okay, perhaps not the coffee), whilst poor decisions erode capital. Organisational futures are determined to a material extent by the decisions made by the leaders responsible for their operations.

Having served in multi-billion-dollar organisations at senior levels for over twenty years, I have watched as organisational decision-making has evolved. The closer I've got to high-stakes decisions, the more fascinated I've become by how they are made in practice. I have watched egos drive decisions that have made little rational sense, watched as a lack of imagination has destroyed brilliant ideas, and equally, watched as seemingly unfathomable decisions have created significant shareholder wealth. I've often wondered what shareholders would think if they were a fly on the wall.

Before we move on, it's worth spending a bit of time looking at the theory that underpins organisational decision-making.

Organisational Theory

Organisations can be thought of as legal fictions,[21] constructs that allow us to separate a metaphysical legal entity from both the individuals who run it and those who own it. At their core, organisations are a complex network of written and unwritten contracts among various stakeholders. Each party enters this network aiming to maximise their own interests, whether that be profit, job satisfaction, value creation, or otherwise.

Although some would disagree, capital organisations fundamentally exist to create wealth for their owners. Without the prospect of generating a return on investment, organisations would simply not exist outside of the not-for-profit sector. If we borrow once again from economics, the purpose of an organisation is to maximise

21 JENSEN, M. C. & MECKLING, W. H. 1976. Theory of the firm: Managerial behavior, agency costs and ownership structure. *Journal of Financial Economics*, 3, 305-360.

utility for its owners by making optimal choices that grow invested capital. Let's explore the practical challenges.

Sole traders are the best example of simple organisational structures where decisions align naturally with the owner's interests. In the sole proprietor model, owners are synonymous with their business, and there is no legal separation between the two. That's not to say that decisions will always be good ones, simply that there is no potential conflict between the organisation and the owner's wishes. As ever, decisions will be bounded by access to information, temporal limitations, and cognitive ability.

Limited companies, by contrast, enable owners to separate themselves legally from their company. The company enters into commitments and holds the majority of the legal liability. In the event of a dispute, legally, the dispute is between the company and the customer, not the owner and the customer. This may seem like a trivial point, but it is an important one and one that is easily overlooked. Legally, in most constructs, an organisation is separate from its owner.

Agency Conflict

As organisations grow, and particularly once they invite outside shareholders, complexity rises rapidly. Publicly listed companies are amongst the most complex in this regard. Although the original founder may manage to keep a healthy percentage of voting rights, ownership becomes distributed across a far wider range of people and institutions. Aligning interests among these stakeholders can be challenging.

For the large part however, what is in the interests of one shareholder ought to be in the interests of all, but it is not necessarily the case. Activist venture capitalists, for example, wield their voting power and influence in a manner that is likely to ruffle feathers and may push for shorter-term returns than the average shareholder. They typically seek to take an active role in the company's management, with most pushing for board seats. They are rarely welcomed by the executive teams of the organisations they invest in. That said, from an economic perspective at least, whilst the methods may differ, all else being equal, the financial interests of shareholders ought to be broadly served by their involvement.

The biggest challenge for organisations as they grow is that decisions become separated from the company's ownership. As companies scale, they devolve accountability for day-to-day operational decisions to leadership teams and staff. Agency challenges occur where the interests of such staff are misaligned with the owners. Anyone who has spent any time in an organisation is familiar with this challenge. Aligning interests and incentives has been a preoccupation among academics and practitioners for decades.

Day-to-day decisions are delegated to employees, typically within a schedule of authority, outlining the decisions and decision parameters that can be made at various levels in the organisation. Such documents cover everything from the approval of travel expenses to the authority to commit to material capital expenditure. Invariably the board is the ultimate approver, trumping the CEO as a decision-making authority. Fundamentally, the intention of such governance schemes is to make decisions at a level appropriate to the decision's potential impact - with the highest stakes decisions left to the board and, in some instances, to a shareholder vote.

The primary purpose of the modern board is to ensure that the CEO and associated leadership team run the organisation and make decisions in the interests of shareholders. Admittedly, there are some unusual constructs, particularly in the US, where chairman and CEO positions are combined (for reasons that defy any logic that I've ever been able to discern), but in the vast majority of instances, non-executive directors are charged with independently overseeing high-stakes decisions. The board is intended to be independent of the executive team and have legal responsibility for its macro performance.

However, the average board member spends less than 10% of their time in support of the organisations they oversee. Historically there has been massive information asymmetry between boards and executive teams. Board packs are produced to support major decisions, and insight is provided into material obligations. On the back of such information, the board is expected to act as the commercial conscience of the shareholders. In real terms, the board are always going to be massively influenced by the information they are provided and the way it is presented. Consider the framing effect we highlighted previously.

It always struck me as ironic that an organisation's ultimate governance body has such a narrow view of operations. It is the equivalent of looking at a room from the wrong side of a keyhole. Not only is the view ridiculously narrow but to extend our analogy further, imagine that the keyhole can be manipulated from the inside to change the view of the room that is provided.

Clearly, most executives will not set out to deceive. But there are certainly examples that spring readily to mind of occasions where the opposite has been true. Enron is perhaps the most cited example of corporate governance failure. In that instance, the executive team was hiding in plain sight, and anyone with a cursory understanding of cash flow, balance sheet, and profit and loss should have quickly unpicked the creative narrative being spun. However, they failed to do so.

The economic theory of organisational decision-making is not wholly dissimilar to that which we explored when considering human decision-making. Optimal decisions require an exhaustive search for alternatives, rationally objective assessment, and maximising utility.

However, in most real-world organisations, search is limited; in other words, exploring a relatively modest number of options is the only practicable option. Assessment is often hugely subjective, and decisions as ever satisfice as opposed to optimise. Information asymmetry between the originator and the approver reduces transparency and creates malleable situations.

For centuries, there has been no viable alternative to the flawed model we've just outlined. However, the situation has begun to change. Many decisions can now be automated.

Automated Organisational Decisions

When I started my career, almost every purchase requisition had to be manually reviewed and converted to a purchase order. Invoices were manually sent, received, and validated against both purchase orders and acknowledgement from the requisitioner that they had received the associated goods/services. Standing armies of people in low-cost locations were responsible for facilitating the process and making countless micro-decisions in a prescribed format. Fortunately for all concerned, most organisations have now automated the process and associated decision-making.

However, countless decisions are still made every day within organisations manually. Typically, the higher-stakes the decision, the more manual the process. Technology is beginning to emerge for the first time, which may address this balance while reducing information asymmetry in the bargain. The challenge, as ever, is where to deploy such technology, where to leverage human talent, and where to adopt a hybrid model.

While many papers, articles, and books discuss this issue, very few, if any, provide a practical model to frame the debate. The following model attempts to redress this balance.

Key Takeaways

- Agency issues arise where ownership becomes separated from management as companies grow
- Various mechanisms including the appointment of boards established to manage agency conflict and align incentives between shareholders and management
- Significant historical information asymmetry between boards and management teams
- Organisational decisions are bounded by the same limitations as human decision-making including cognitive limitations, lack of time, and imperfect search for alternatives
- Organisational decisions satisfice rather than optimise
- Lack of alternatives historically to organic decision-making,

but the situation is rapidly changing on the back of automation

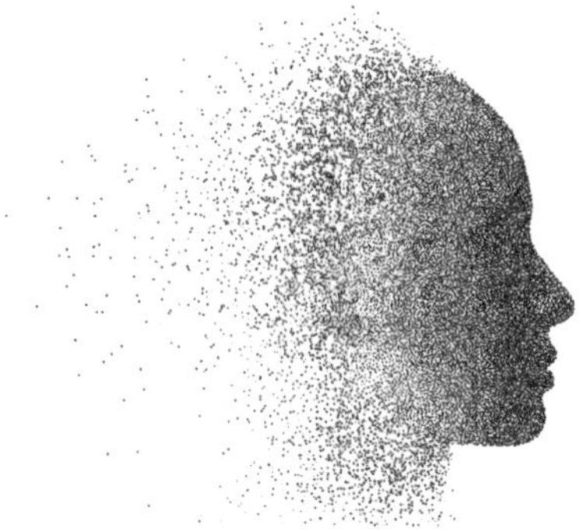

Chapter 6

A Model for Practice

"An idea that is developed and put into action is more important than an idea that exists only as an idea."

Edward De Bono - Physician

~ A Model For Practice ~

From the earliest days of my career, I became fascinated by the interplay between technology, human talent, and organisational decision-making. As a commercial leader, I have seen the best and worst of both worlds over the years. I've watched as technology has been deployed with the intention of streamlining decisions, only to fail at the slightest deviation between code and reality. I've watched leaders make decisions that have destroyed shareholder value in one instance while making decisions that have transformed a stock's performance in another.

In a dynamic world, I have always felt that there's a place for both humans and technology in organisational decision-making. The challenge has always been how to strike a balance between the two.

The following model is based on discussions with C-suite leaders, board members, and advisory firms covering multiple industries and functional areas. The discussions were part of the qualitative work performed in support of my doctorate with the University of Warwick. As a Chief Procurement Officer in an FTSE100 company, I was privileged to have access to C-suite leaders with significant decision-making authority.

The insight from these conversations has been reflected in the model itself. With a limited number of exceptions, I have deliberately used well-cited examples to protect the identity of the individuals involved in my qualitative research and to make the content more relatable to the average reader. The model was tested and refined based on feedback from partners at two of the world's largest consulting firms.

The model is not intended to provide absolutes but rather to stimulate thought in a structured manner. We identify three decision zones, their characteristics, and the optimal approach to exploiting each. The decision zones are intended to help organisational leaders make well-informed decisions about their investments in technology, human talent, and the associated accelerators.

Even the most optimistic of Luddites would surely acknowledge that machines will continue to encroach into human domains. The question is how far they will go and what inhibitors they are likely to face. We will also address the latter to help future-proof our model.

In the coming pages, we will review the model together with each of its component parts. Annex I outlines how the model can be used in practice.

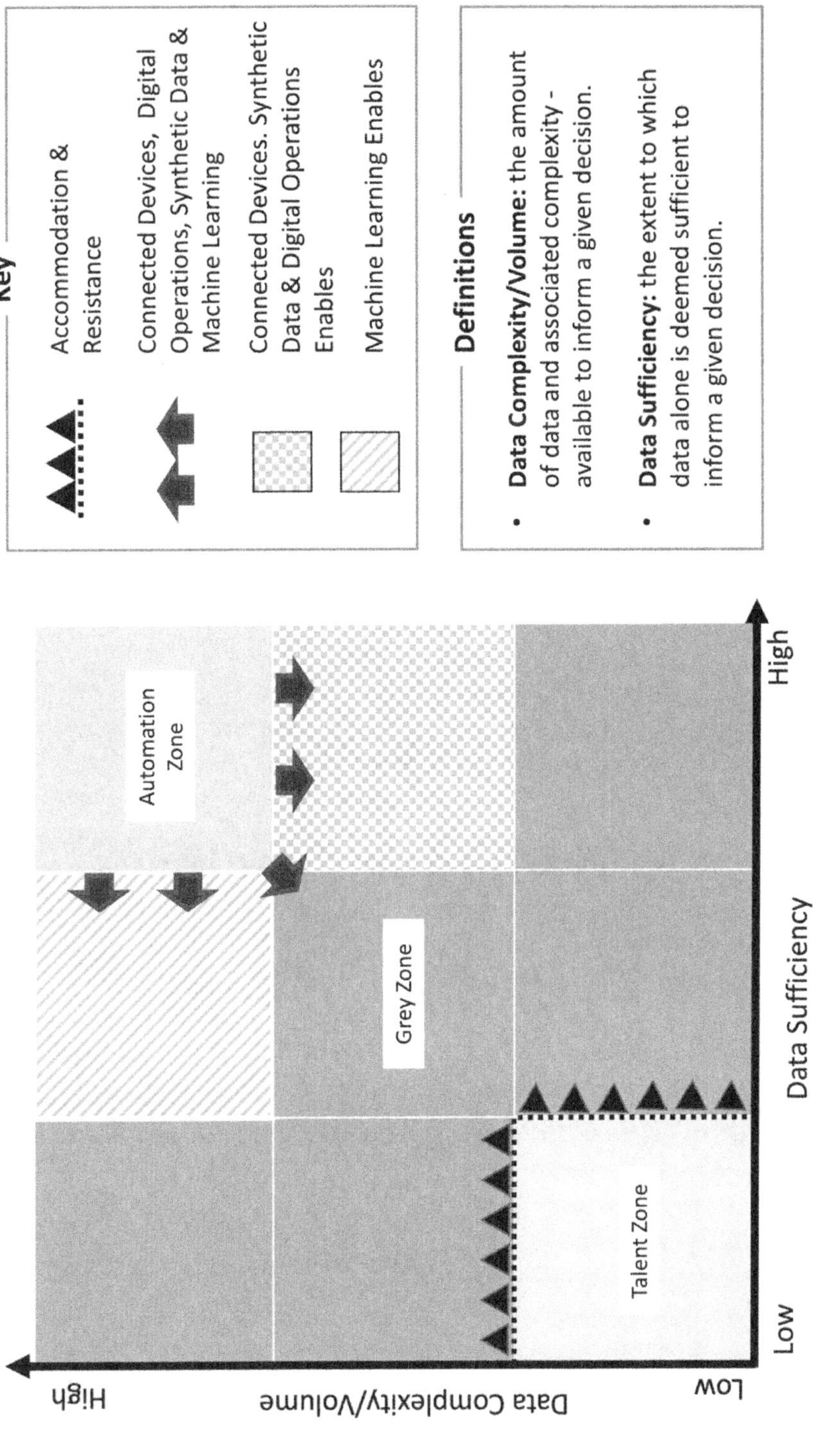
Key
Accommodation & Resistance
Connected Devices, Digital Operations, Synthetic Data & Machine Learning
Connected Devices. Synthetic Data & Digital Operations Enables
Machine Learning Enables
Definitions
Data Complexity/Volume: the amount of data and associated complexity - available to inform a given decision.
Data Sufficiency: the extent to which data alone is deemed sufficient to inform a given decision.
Automation Zone
Grey Zone
Talent Zone
Data Complexity/Volume
High
Low
Data Sufficiency
Low
High

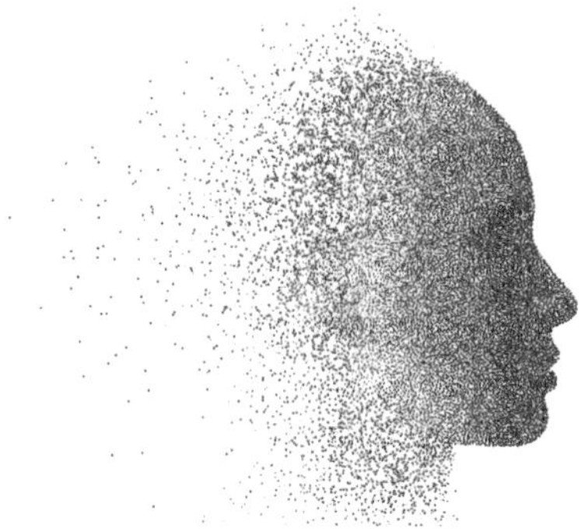

Chapter 7

A Model for Practice:

Criticality of Data

"Data is a precious thing and will last longer than the systems themselves."

Tim Berners-Lee

~ Criticality of Data ~

In the modern organisation, data isn't just a byproduct of operations; it fuels automation and drives actionable insight. I was invited by the CEO of a private equity fund to imagine data as the *oil of the digital age*. Raw and unrefined, data is of limited use, but once processed, it becomes invaluable - powering innovation and driving efficiency. Incidentally, I was subsequently chastised by partners from two consultancy firms for using the same analogy, given the negative connotations associated with oil! Despite risking their chagrin, it still feels like a very apt analogy to me.

According to the International Data Corporation (IDC) report,[22] the global datasphere was estimated at 45 zettabytes in 2018 and projected to grow to 175 zettabytes by 2025. For reference, a zettabyte has 21 zeros! The World Economic Forum anticipates that 463 exabytes of data will be created *every day* by 2025.[23] An exabyte

---

22 IDC, 2018 REINSEL, D., GANTZ, J. & RYDNING, J. 2018. *The Digitization of the World From Edge to Core*.

23 2023. How responsible data can help us navigate the economic crisis. https://www.weforum.org/agenda/2023/01/davos23-responsible-data-protection-economic-crisis/: World Economic Forum.

contains three fewer zeros – but it is a heady number nonetheless and an indication of how rapidly data is growing.

Data informs both axes of our model. Before we get into the guts of our decision zones, it is worth reflecting on the rapid growth of data and its transformative effect on industry.

Data Driven Digital Disruption

When I was growing up, music was expensive and relatively scarce. Local music shops had a limited selection, and I had friends who would travel for miles in the hope of finding a particular album. I remember traipsing to London to visit the new Virgin Megastore on Oxford Street and marvelling at the sheer volume and variety of music available. However, even then, it was still a lottery as to whether the CD you wanted would be available. It was common to visit friends' houses to look at their music collection and listen to hard-to-source tracks.

Skip forward less than forty years, and the music industry has been completely transformed. Streaming services now provide free and unlimited access to huge back catalogues. The ownership model has changed, with consumers now subscribing to on-demand services rather than buying discs. Recording artist's fortunes are now determined as much, if not more, by digital downloads and streams than physical purchases. The barriers to entry have reduced significantly for both producers and aspiring musicians.

While enthusiasts still collect music as a hobby, it is now possible to listen to almost any song for fractions of the historical cost. The music industry serves as a use case for digital disruption. It was also a use case that, for a long time, no one really saw coming. Why?

If asked the question, most people would probably point to Sean Parker and Napster. It's a fair response, but wrong. Napster may have been an early pioneer of streaming services, but they were not the catalyst.

Unless you've read *How Music Got Free,*[24] you will likely never have heard of Dell Glover, a factory worker at a CD manufacturing plant in North Carolina. Glover, however, was perhaps more directly responsible for the disruption of the music industry than any other single figure in history. By stealing pre-release CDs from the production line and distributing them through a network called Rabid Neurosis, Glover became one of the most prolific music pirates in history.

Had Glover merely copied his pilfered music to discs using a traditional CD burner, the world would likely look slightly different today. Reproduction costs would have been significant, and physical distribution would have limited his reach. He would have made a few quid selling music to friends and a small local network, and the industry would barely have noticed.

The catalyst however for the disruption of an entire industry was the fact that his illicit activity coincided with the availability of MP3 technology. The technology allowed software to convert CDs into high-quality MP3 files. These tools allowed for efficient compression without significant loss of sound quality, making the

24 WITT, S. 2015. How Music Got Free: The End of an Industry, The Turn of the Century, and the Patient Zero of Piracy. Viking PR.

files suitable for online sharing. MP3 libraries became extensive in relatively rapid order, fuelled by Glover's piracy.

Digital copies of music with no incremental production costs could be distributed globally in vast quantities, providing the fuel for streaming services such as Napster to exploit. The rest is history, but it was arguably built on the foundations of one man, who perhaps unwittingly digitised what had been a largely physical industry. Incidentally, without such libraries the iPod would not have been possible, and Apple's fortunes would have looked very different.

There are countless analogous examples of how physical assets have become digitised. In 1996, at university, if I wanted to read a particular text, my options were limited to sitting in the library or photocopying vast chunks of physical text to read at my leisure. Both options were, of course, predicated on the book being available in the first place. It was a first-mover advantage to have early access to reading lists, and it was fun to watch the more enthusiastic members of my classes running across campus to get to the books first. Seems funny to imagine now, but at the time, the only way of checking whether a book was available was to visit the library and use the on-premise system.

By the time I was studying for my MBA in 2008, resources were slightly more digital, but enterprising lecturers would still do very well financially by mandating the purchase of their textbooks, and scholarship was still limited by available resources.

Skip forward a few more years to my doctorate in 2018 and pretty much every resource I needed to conduct my research was available online. Instant access through electronic databases reduced search time and cost whilst increasing accessibility to the point where very few texts were beyond my almost immediate reach. Access to information, proximity to libraries, and the ability to perform extensive manual research were no longer differentiators for academics. Of course, expectations rose accordingly, and the average student is now expected to perform far more extensive literature reviews than in the past.

The secondary market has seen pirated copies of almost every textbook and academic paper ever written become available to students for pennies on the pound. Let's face it: younger generations have little love or respect for copyright. Having worked at the world's largest educational publisher, I witnessed the financial impact of the transformation first-hand.

In industry, the same phenomenon has been ongoing for years. I worked as a commercial manager in my first job at the turn of the century. If I wanted to review a particular client contract, I would fill in a physical form and go down to see the sartorially elegant record keeper in the basement. Standing a constant vigil over rows of perfectly filed contracts, I would wait as he reviewed my slip, looked at me suspiciously, and disappeared into the archives. It was more than my life was worth to misplace said contract. The contract was likely one of only two in existence and physically signed in ink.

Today, of course, most contracts are maintained digitally. Contracts are signed in tools such as DocuSign and stored in the cloud. Contract databases enable authorised users to access documentation instantly from anywhere in the world, search the documents using keywords, and view all previous iterations.

At the time, contracts were not the only physical manifestations of our craft. Business cases were printed, walked around the floors, and signed by the great and good. Notes on negotiations were kept in lever arch files and stored for prosperity. An erstwhile admin assistant would record and print meeting minutes for future reference. The result was an elaborate paper trail that outlined the evolution of a particular transaction and resulted in mountains of physical but largely inaccessible data.

In the unfortunate case of a contractual dispute, lawyers would pour over physical files. Paperwork would emerge from various sources across the world, creating mountains of evidence to be reviewed. The process of finding a *silver bullet* was laborious and largely manual. Of course, it is easy to make physical evidence disappear, and I suspect shredders got a healthy amount of exercise back in the day.

The situation has changed nowadays. Email, instant messages, documents, business cases, and minutes are all available digitally. Pretty much everything leaves a trace and more importantly creates digital data. Legal discovery has been reduced to a far more efficient digital process, and removing evidence is considerably harder without leaving a trail somewhere in the ether.

Abstracting from documents, it was only a decade ago that if I wanted to know how many staff were in the office, I would have asked a member of the real estate team to walk around and count the number of physical heads. Nowadays sensors and entry badges tell me when people are in, how long they are in for, and where they sit during their time in the office. Estate planning is somewhat more efficient when this information can be pulled up instantly to inform plans.

It's fair to say then that organisations are creating more data than at any point in the past. With increasingly digital operations and the deployment of smart sensors, the physical world is increasingly reduced to bits and bytes.

One consequence of the proliferation of data is a clear move toward data-driven decision-making. Companies are investing heavily in data capabilities, recognising that solid information and insights derived from data analysis lead to better decisions. Executive teams and boards expect ever higher-quality data to inform choices.

In the media industry, data analytics is revolutionising content creation and strategy. Editors once decided on stories based on personal judgement and experience. Now, they calculate the return on investment for every story, analysing which pieces generate the most value across advertising, subscriptions, and commerce. A friend and colleague of mine, now serving as a Chief Information Officer in the media sector, explained how data-driven insights are guiding editorial decisions, ensuring resources are focused on content that resonates with audiences and drives revenue. Much of this insight is derived in real-time.

The rise of wearable devices provides organisations with unprecedented insights into consumer habits and health. Fitness trackers and smartwatches collect data on physical activity, sleep patterns, and heart rate. This data not only empowers consumers to make healthier lifestyle choices but also offers valuable information to healthcare providers and insurers looking to promote wellness programs. We can't be too far away from barely needing to articulate symptoms to a doctor, because they will already have the information at hand. The days of filling out a questionnaire about drinking and smoking habits will become superfluous. That is, of course, assuming that you can get an appointment with a doctor in the first place!

Several members of my university cohort currently work in healthcare, with one holding a senior position at a global pharmaceutical company and another serving as the CEO and owner of one of the largest private hospitals in the Middle East. The former's research explores the rise of preventative life science practices to proactively promote better health, while the latter explores the use of lean methodologies in a hospital setting. Both rely heavily on the vast amount of data being created for the first time.

However, not all data is equally valuable, and its importance can change over time. Data's molecular value varies based on context, relevance, and timeliness.

COVID-19 demonstrated how the value of data can shift dramatically. Historical data patterns suddenly became less predictive as consumer behaviours and market conditions changed in response to lockdown and the associated physical restrictions. Retailers, for example, found that supply chain forecasts based on pre-pandemic data were no longer accurate. Companies had to adjust their models and strategies to account for these sudden shifts, highlighting the need for data analysis and decision-making agility.

By contrast, real-time data became immensely valuable. Supermarket chains analysed purchasing trends to manage inventory, while health authorities used mobility data to track the spread of the virus and inform public health decisions. One of the things that surprised me during the pandemic, however, was the vastly different conclusions drawn by health authorities based on the same data sets! An interesting topic in and of itself.

Data Volume & Complexity

For the purposes of decision making, two critical variables are associated with data. The first is the sheer volume and complexity of the data produced by an organisation. As volume increases and the data collected becomes less and less structured, it becomes harder for human cognition to process at speed. It becomes a diminishing return for organisations to deploy human agents to process data to extract insights and is beyond their temporal and cognitive ability to sustain over long periods. Technology becomes a prerequisite for dealing with volume.

Consider the serious fraud office. In a world where, as we have highlighted, almost everything leaves physical traces, fraud detection involves unimaginable amounts of data from disparate sources in disparate forms. It would be impracticable to attempt to manage modern-day complexity with traditional methods. Technology becomes an effective *coping* mechanism.

Thus, *data volume and complexity* become essential variables when considering potential decision-making use cases. We recognise this in the first axis of our model.

Data Sufficiency

That said, not all data is of equal value in decision-making. Organisations create rafts of data that have limited practical application in making informed decisions. Equally, not all decisions can be purely informed by hard data.

Two of the most critical decisions made by organisations concern who to hire and where to deploy scarce capital. Let's start with the former.

Despite everything that has changed in recent years, CVs still serve as the primary vehicle for organisations to screen potential employees. Historically, recruiters reviewed these CVs alongside cover letters, and based on their professional judgement, a selection would be passed to a hiring manager. An interview process would then take place, and a decision would be made.

Increasingly providers encourage us to think about the process with a far more automated mindset. Technology can screen CVs, promising to remove bias, and even overlay information with internet searches, marrying publicly available sources with the information relayed by the candidate.

However, even with perfect information, very few of us would likely allow a machine to make a hiring decision on our behalf. Cultural fit, chemistry, and a raft of other subjective factors feature in our decision-making. It is often claimed that most hiring managers know within 30 seconds of meeting someone whether they are likely to hire them.

By way of illustration, I once sat in my manager's office on the first day of a new role I'd been hired for. He'd carelessly left on his desk, some of his interview notes. Without prying, my eyes were drawn to a comparison table between myself and two of my competitors. The first row detailed the relative merits of our respective handshakes. Apparently, mine was firm and accompanied by good eye contact. One of my competitors was limp. At the time, it made me laugh. However, the point is that regardless of whether it is a physical cue or some other subjective factor, hard data is typically insufficient to make a hiring decision, although it may well inform it.

Capital allocation decisions are amongst the highest-stakes decisions made by organisations. Whether to invest in a particular asset or capability, buy or divest an organisation, or return cash to shareholders are critical success factors for organisations. Such decisions are informed by rafts of data, and many leaders will talk about making data-driven decisions in this regard.

However, the reality is that in many instances, the highest stakes decisions, whilst informed by data involve significant amounts of subjective input. Assessing a company on paper is one thing. You can understand the fundamentals of the business, derive a myriad of financial ratios, and use that insight to compare alternatives. However, what the quantitative analysis can't tell you is the nature of the organisational culture, the talent inherent amongst the personnel, the quality of the customer relationships, and the longevity of the associated market. All these things call for judgement and experience.

Whilst we address the consequences of this further in due course, suffice for now to highlight that *data sufficiency* is the second key variable of our model. In other words, the degree to which data is a sufficient basis to make a particular decision.

Summary: Criticality of Data

Enabler	Considerations
Data Volume/Complexity – scale of data and complexity across unstructured, semi-structured and structured data	• Volume of data growing exponentially through connected devices and digital operations • Closed loop processes may enable zero touch or lights out processes • Robust data strategy required to collect and exploit data in an ethical manner • Not all data is of equal value and such value changes over time
Data Sufficiency – extent to which data is sufficient to make decisions	• Consider extent to which rational decisions can be repeated at scale against hard decision logic • Machine learning may impact, and increase data sufficiency • Consider value of subjective criteria in decision making – to what extent does it differentiate

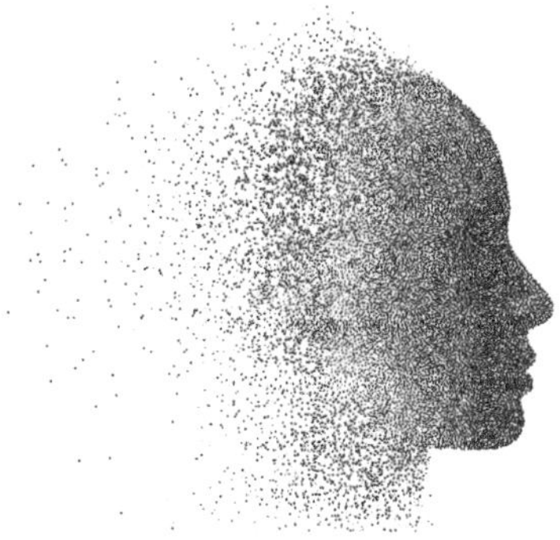

Chapter 8

A Model for Practice: Automation Zone

"I do not fear computers. I fear the lack of them."

Isaac Asimov

~ Automation Zone ~

Organisations are increasingly creating and storing structured, semi-structured, and unstructured data at unprecedented volumes. As data increases in volume and complexity, machines become the only commercially viable method of *coping* with the associated scale. Human cognitive and temporal limitations render even the brightest minds moot in the face of such enormity.

Where this volume and complexity is accompanied by high levels of data sufficiency, machines serve as perfectly adapted decision-making agents. As a reminder, data sufficiency refers to decisions that can be made solely on the basis of data. Such decisions typically exhibit high degrees of repeatability and are formulaic in nature.

At the extreme of our model then, machines serve as *coping pioneers*.

Coping Mechanisms

Take fraud detection, which has become vital as the volume of global financial transactions grows exponentially. The sheer scale of data that needs to be monitored for fraudulent activity is immense. Visa, for instance, reportedly processes over 65,000 transaction messages per second, handling more than 150 million transactions daily across its network.[25] Each of these transactions must be scrutinised in near real-time to detect and prevent fraudulent activity.

According to the Association of Certified Fraud Examiners (ACFE), organisations worldwide lose an estimated 5% of their annual revenues to fraud, with potential global losses of over $5 trillion.[26] Without machines, it would be impractical to cover anything other than the most severe instances of fraud, and even then, at a glacial pace. That said, the challenge still doesn't make me any more sympathetic to the fact that my credit card gets cancelled every time I travel somewhere slightly off-piste!

In a like manner, high-frequency trading (HFT), a form of algorithmic trading where huge volumes of transactions are executed at high speed, often within fractions of a second, would be impossible without significant compute. HFT firms utilise complex algorithms to analyse multiple markets and execute split-second orders based on market conditions. Whilst the holy grail of risk-free arbitrage remains out of reach in the near term, HFT aims to capitalise on small price discrepancies that exist for mere microseconds. Trades can be executed in less than one millisecond enabling organisations to take advantage of favourable trading conditions.

In both examples, data volumes are unimaginably large, and highly repeatable decision logic can be applied to optimise decisions.

---

25 Visa Inc. 2024 Investor Relations https://investor.visa.com

26 2024. OCCUPATIONAL FRAUD 2024: A REPORT TO THE NATIONS https://legacy.acfe.com/report-to-the-nations/2024/.

While the transactions are overseen by human agents at a macro level, they are largely closed-loop systems. Closed-loop systems refer to decision-making environments where all the necessary data required to make a decision is captured in a digital ecosystem without requiring input or interference from outside factors. It is impossible to imagine that human operators could ever replicate the capability of such machines. In the case of Visa, transactions would be far slower, and fraud far more prevalent. In the case of HFT, the industry simply would not exist.

In retail, Walmart serves as an exemplar of the need to manage scale and complexity. On a weekly basis circa 240 million shoppers visit Walmart's 10,500 stores. With over 100,000 suppliers, a reported 150 distribution centres and a myriad of transport types to manage, operating at scale involves some heroic numbers! A combination of AI and machine learning within an in-house developed system, Element, has enabled the retailer to enhance channel performance, improve customer search functionality, drive market insight, and enhance last-mile delivery.[27] Customer tolerance for arriving at stores to find that items are not in stock is low, and the ability to deal efficiently with scale in a competitive market is a critical success factor.

Similarly, ride-hailing systems call for a delicate balance between supply and demand. Again, the scale is enormous, with Uber reportedly processing over 2.8 billion rides in Q2 of 2024 alone. Systems need to be capable of anticipating demand, ensuring

27 Walmart Inc., 2024 https://stock.walmart.com/home/default.aspx

adequate driver coverage, accurately estimating time, distance, and cost, and collecting real-time feedback on driver performance.

In recent years, dynamic pricing has been introduced by Uber and others, complicating the matter further. Dynamic pricing helps to ensure that drivers attend areas seeing a surge in demand and ensures that drivers make themselves available at anti-social hours in return for suitable premium fares. The ability to dynamically adjust tariffs based on real-time insight has become a competitive necessity in an increasingly crowded market. The systems employ a mix of AI and machine learning to drive algorithmic decision-making that combines geospatial, temporal, and market data. In traditional taxi firms, call operators would simply dispatch cars on demand, but at circa 1 billion rides a month, the efficient use of technology is the only practical way to deal with the associated scale.

Machines as Pioneers

In addition to serving as effective *coping* mechanisms, machines are critically able to identify trends, patterns, and opportunities across vast data sets in a way that would be beyond human cognitive ability.

In 2016, Moorfields Eye Hospital took part in a first-of-a-kind pilot with Google DeepMind with a view to revolutionising eye care and promoting earlier detection of retinal disease. A dataset of over one million anonymised retinal scans, one of the largest ophthalmic imaging data sets in the world, was used to train DeepMind's AI system. In the final synopsis, the system could identify over 50 different eye conditions with a 94% accuracy rate. Moorfields handles over 700,000 patient visits annually, with the resultant technology materially reducing the time between referral and treatment.[28]

While that may be remarkable, perhaps the more interesting aspect of the pilot for our purposes, was the study's unintended consequences. By running machine learning across the data set, researchers were able to identify subtle markers enabling the accurate prediction of cardiovascular disease. The system was able to reliably detect age, blood pressure, and smoking status - serving as an accurate early indicator of stroke and heart conditions. The detection of such patterns would have been beyond the most gifted of medical practitioners and completely impractical to repeat accurately at scale. The implications for the healthcare and insurance industry are immense.

In a like manner, Trafton[29] reports that researchers at the Massachusetts Institute of Technology (MIT) used machine learning to identify a new antibiotic compound capable of destroying disease-causing bacteria that had proven impervious to extant treatments. The researchers named the new compound halicin, a playful take on the AI system, from *2001: A Space Odyssey*. Feels appropriate, given that the potential new wonder drug was only discovered after analysing over 100 million chemical compounds. Whilst using technology for drug discovery is far from a new concept, historic efforts have largely proved unreliable. Recent advances in neural networks and pattern recognition led to the pioneering breakthrough.

28 https://moorfieldsbrc.nihr.ac.uk

29 TRAFTON, A. 2020. Artificial intelligence yields new antibiotic. https://news.mit.edu/2020/artificial-intelligence-identifies-new-antibiotic-0220.

A Cautionary Note

Whilst there are undoubtedly commercial benefits to be exploited by using machines as coping pioneers, organisations should actively consider a number of issues. Not least of which is to avoid deploying technology for the sake of it. Deploying technology, particularly AI, simply because it is available, and ticks a box, is not a great strategy.

Where machines process data against explicit, repeatable rules, risks are mitigated, though not eliminated. Take, for example, a credit decision at a bank. A highly repeatable, rational decision predicated on the applicant's credit history, income, expenditure and nature of the associated purchase. However, consider a 90-year-old widow who is applying to renew their mortgage. Rationally, the credit decision may be rejected, but from a reputational perspective, would the bank want the publicity associated with evicting a grandmother of three from their home? I suspect not.

Organisations should consider applying human oversight to decisions, even where those decisions are being made at high speed and across significant volumes. In days gone by, credit decisions would be referred to increasingly senior underwriters. A digital equivalent needs to be considered for certain high-risk scenarios. In regulatory environments such as financial services, this is mandatory in a number of instances, but organisational discretion plays a greater role in other industries.

The situation, however, becomes much more complicated when AI and machine learning are involved. Borrowing from the EU AI Act, which we cover in greater detail in Chapter 12, we can define AI as machines that infer decisions and recommendations from implicit rules, operate autonomously, and are capable of adaptiveness.

The challenge from the definition alone should be apparent. Inference suggests that a machine has some degree of latitude regarding how decisions are made. Therefore, the notion of machine learning is inherent in the definition. Given that the machine may operate without human oversight and owing to its adaptive potential, the underlying logic may quickly become opaque. Organisations should pay close attention to transparency, explainability, and only permit autonomous adaptation with extreme care.

The data and training methods used to inform algorithms and parameters governing its adaptiveness are of critical concern. While humans are prone to bias, machines, whilst technically impartial, have the potential to demonstrate extreme bias at scale predicated on the nature of the data used to train and refine their algorithms. The challenge for deploying organisations is ensuring that they have adequate insight into these commercially sensitive areas. The risks are, however, obvious.

The Correctional Offender Management Profiling for Alternative Sanctions (COMPAS) system deployed in the US to support automated parole and sentencing decisions serves as a case in point. An independent investigation by ProPublica, as reported in Harvard Law Review,[30] suggests that the system, which analyses a defendant's likelihood of reoffending, was inherently biased leading

30 2017. Wisconsin Supreme Court Requires Warning Before Use of Algorithmic Risk Assessments in Sentencing. 5 ed. https://harvardlawreview.org/print/vol-130/state-v-loomis/: Harvard Law Review.

to socially significant consequences.

ProPublica's findings suggested that the COMPAS tool correctly predicted recidivism in a mere 61% of cases – slightly better than the toss of a coin. However, black defendants were identified as high risk twice as often as they actually reoffended, whereas the reverse was true of their white counterparts:

	White Defendants	Black American Defendants
Labelled Higher Risk, But Didn't Re-Offend	23.5%	44.9%
Labelled Lower Risk, Yet Did Re-Offend	47.7%	28.0%

It is troubling, to say the least, that a system with a proprietary algorithmic logic and confidential training set was ever approved for use in the judicial system, particularly in a country that has a troubled history regarding the treatment of certain demographics.

Interestingly, the system was challenged by Eric Loomis following his arrest for offences related to a drive-by shooting incident in 2013 in Winconsin. During his sentencing, the court used COMPAS to evaluate his likelihood of recidivism. He was sentenced to six years. Loomis subsequently filed a motion arguing that his rights had been violated given that he had been denied access to the algorithm used to calculate his risk score - preventing him from challenging its accuracy and fairness.

In 2016, the Wisconsin Supreme Court ruled against the defendant. The court held that while the algorithm was proprietary, Loomis had been provided with sufficient information to challenge the scoring and that, in any event, the court had the right to exercise discretion over the system's recommendation, which was intended to serve as a guide.

The system remains in use today.

Practical Management

As we highlight in Chapter 12, legislation is emerging to protect the worst abuses of technology. However, it is nascent at best. Pro-innovation regimes are reticent to inhibit access to technology. Those who have taken a more stringent approach, most notably the EU, focus the majority of obligations on suppliers. However, for large commercial organisations, the risk, in real terms will sit with deployers of such solutions.

Rather than wait for legislation to catch up or avoid falling behind the curve from a technology perspective, the following six guiding principles can serve as a useful practical guide.

- Data Governance

  As we have observed, data fuels automation generally, but AI, and in particular, LLMs, love data! Establishing policies, standards, and procedures to ensure that data is collected, stored, and used appropriately is essential given its role in training AI systems and powering post-deployment adaptability.

- Explainability

  Explainability refers to the ability to understand the rationale underpinning the output from AI systems. Given that AI is increasingly used to inform high-stakes decisions, it is critical to understand how such decisions have been made. That said, there is a potential trade-off between the performance of so-called black-box systems and those with transparent architectures. Stanford University reported that, at present, the former materially outperforms the latter.[31]

- Transparency

Transparency concerns the degree of insight available to users into key design choices, including data sources, training methods, and algorithmic logic. Given that such systems are often adaptive post-deployment, transparency is also a key principle once they are in operational use.

- Privacy

Privacy concerns the use of personal and sensitive data and a user's right to anonymity. These are not new concepts. They are, however, materially impacted by the use of AI. Advanced AI may enable users to be identified from anonymised data, whilst new use cases result in the collection of data in novel ways that could potentially be exploited (consider care bots for example, automated companions that are used to converse with the elderly and sick).

- Fairness

Fairness largely involves removing bias and ensuring that

31 Artificial Intelligence Index Report 2024. AI Index Report 2024 – Artificial Intelligence Index.

algorithms reflect societal norms concerning freedom and basic human rights. This is particularly pertinent in relation to areas such as the justice system, medicine, and education, where ensuring fair and equitable access is critical. Data governance, privacy, and transparency all play significant roles in ensuring that algorithms are representative and fair.

- Security & Safety

  Again, security and safety are not new concepts. Ensuring that systems are safe and secure is perhaps more critical than ever, given the trust that users are placing in such systems, the sensitivity of the data contained, and the potential for misuse in the event of a malicious attack. Equally, systems themselves are increasingly capable of making high-stakes decisions that can result in the distribution of harm. Autonomous vehicles serve as an obvious example.

In short, establishing a responsible AI capability feels like an increasing necessity for most large organisations.

Summary: Automation Zone

Decision Zone Characteristics	Automation Strategy	Considerations
• High volumes/ complexity of data (structured, semi-structured and unstructured) • High degrees of data sufficiency – where data can be used to drive rational, repeatable decisions based on hard logic	• Machines deployed as coping mechanism • Machines used to pioneer novel ways to exploit data and drive revenue • Promote data democracy • Limit human decision-making – whilst maintaining oversight and transparency • Robust data strategy supported by connected devices and digital operations	• Machine learning may be necessary to maximise value and drive data sufficiency • Organisations should make conscious and well-informed decisions about black-box technology • Consider establishing ethical board to oversee potential societal and reputational impacts • Customer, regulatory, government & professional body accommodation and resistance to be considered and mitigated

Decision Zone Characteristics	Automation Strategy	Considerations
		• Closed loop processes may enable zero touch or lights out processes • Competitive advantage if early adopter, competitive necessity if fast follower • Robust data strategy required to collect and exploit data in an ethical manner

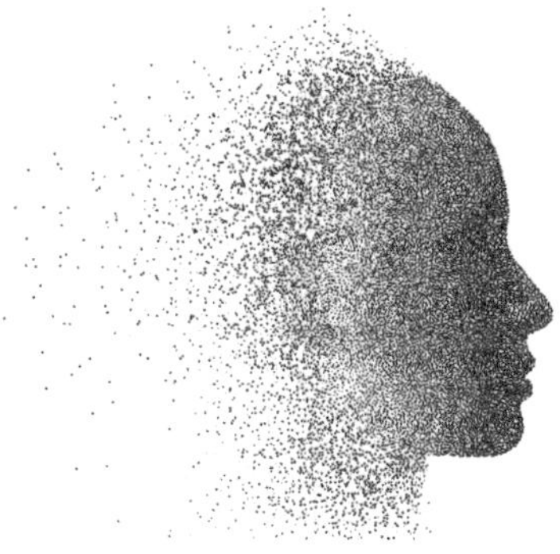

Chapter 9

A Model for Practice:

Talent Zone

"All of my best decisions in business and in life have been made with heart, intuition, and guts, not analysis."

Jeff Bezos

~ Talent Zone ~

In an era increasingly dominated by data analytics, algorithms, and predictive modelling, it is easy to assume that the best organisational decisions will be those supported by hard numbers and linear projections. It is tempting to imagine that technology will dominate organisational decision-making and that data democracy will enable well-informed boards to endorse optimised decisions in double quick time. It would, however, be a mistake to think in such binary terms.

Human Competitive Advantage

Some of the most transformative high-stakes decisions defy convention and data-driven logic. The ability to creatively project the future, combined with the influencing skills, charisma, and sheer force of conviction to inspire others to embrace uncharted paths are uniquely human traits. In most conceivable futures these human traits will continue to differentiate organisations, providing a source of unique and sustainable competitive advantage.

High-stakes decisions often require more than just analytical prowess; they demand creativity, experience, intuition, and the power to galvanise a team behind a bold vision. In many high-stakes decisions, data sufficiency is modest, and information about key subjective elements of transactions is both limited and hard to rationalise.

These factors create engineering bottlenecks that are ill-suited to machines. They are the domain of elite human talent.

Creatively Projecting the Future

Humans possess a remarkable ability to imagine futures that don't logically extend from the present - a non-linear perspective that machines and data models struggle to replicate. This visionary thinking enables leaders to make decisions that, on paper, might seem ill-advised but can ultimately lead to groundbreaking innovation and market shifts.

When Steve Jobs returned to Apple in 1997 after a 12-year absence, the company was on the brink of bankruptcy. Most leaders would likely have played it safe, cutting costs and incrementally improving core products. Jobs had other ideas. Instead, of refining the existing range of personal computers, Jobs developed the iPod.

Introduced in 2001, the iPod marked Apple's first foray into digital music, a departure from its computing foundations. Critics questioned the move. What did a personal computer company know about music? Yet, Jobs saw the potential to integrate hardware, software, and content delivery in a way that no one had imagined at the time. MP3 technology was already in existence when the iPod was released but it was clunky and unsophisticated. The iPod was sleek, fast, beautifully designed, and perhaps most importantly, supported by iTunes. The latter allowed users to create libraries on their personal devices and auto-sync their playlists.

Critically, the iPod's success paved the way for the iPhone in 2007 and the iPad in 2010, devices that didn't just improve existing products but created entirely new ecosystems. The App Store transformed the way that software was built, monetised, and delivered – connecting a network of developers directly with consumers. The phone went from being a functional communication device to a digital Swiss Army Knife. Job's ability to creatively project the future of personal devices in a non-linear manner transformed Apple into one of the world's most valuable companies.

In a like manner Elon Musk's ventures with Tesla and SpaceX epitomise non-linear thinking. When Musk invested in Tesla Motors in 2004, electric vehicles were a niche market, hampered by technological limitations and lacking consumer interest. Traditional manufacturers and investors were sceptical, focusing on incremental improvements to petrol and diesel engines. Musk however, invested heavily in battery technology and manufacturing capabilities, decisions that seemed risky given the company's limited resources and the market's indifference to the technology.

Similarly, Musk's forays with SpaceX are equally gravity-defying (pun intended). Not famed for his crippling lack of self-confidence, Musk's ambition to reach Mars is surely one of the most ambitious aims of any modern-day entrepreneur. Creating reusable rockets to make the project more financially viable was met with derision by many. In 2017, Musk claimed to have already spent over $1 billion on the reusability programme.[32] Whether his long-term aspiration to colonise Mars is met remains to be seen, but his ability to think creatively about the future is surely beyond question.

Both Musk and Job's ability to creatively project non-linear futures and act decisively has propelled Apple, Tesla, and SpaceX to the forefront of their respective industries, illustrating the transformative impact of human talent. Outstanding leaders represent sustainable competitive differentiators for the companies they serve. Their unique human traits are not easily replicated by the competition.

Against this backdrop, consider the core tenets of the Innovator's Dilemma, a book by Harvard professor Clayton Christensen. At risk of oversimplifying, The Innovator's Dilemma describes the challenge facing historically successful organisations when new, disruptive technologies emerge. These companies typically focus on *sustaining innovation* and making incremental improvements to existing products. The result is that their linear progression overshoots customer requirements, resulting in enhancements that have limited market value.

Leaders who overcome the Innovator's Dilemma do so by envisioning non-linear futures and embracing disruptive technologies before they become mainstream. They creatively project a future that defies conventional expectations and rally their organisations to invest in unproven markets and capabilities. This proactive approach requires

32 BROOKE, J. 2017. Elon Musk Spends $1B In Developing Reusable Rockets. https://www.scienceworldreport.com/articles/60085/20170623/elon-musk-spent-1b-developing-reusable-rockets.htm: Science World Report.

a departure from pure data-driven certainty and embracing visionary thinking - hallmarks of human decision-making that machines cannot easily replicate. By anticipating shifts that others overlook and engendering followership around bold strategies, leaders can navigate their organisations through uncertainty to achieve transformative success.

Human Influence

Yet organisations are complex political structures. It is not enough for a leader to have a creative vision of the future; leaders must also find ways to make their vision a reality. Countless so-called strategies fail, not because they are poor ideas but because they can't be operationalised.

Both Jobs and Musk are notoriously challenging leaders, famed for their obsessive personalities, drive, and straight-talking. During critical periods, such as the ramp-up of Tesla's Model 3 production, Musk famously slept at the Tesla factory in Fremont, California. He chose to stay on-site to oversee operations, troubleshoot issues in real-time, and motivate his team to meet ambitious production targets. Jobs, in turn, was known to call meetings at all hours and would tirelessly iterate on prototypes until they met his exacting functional and aesthetic standards. Whilst both have attracted a heady mix of detractors, they had followership in spades. People gravitate towards such leaders and go the extra mile to make extraordinary things happen.

Very few leaders can make high-stakes decisions in isolation from the board and their shareholders. Even with substantial personal shareholdings, corporate governance requires that major capital investment decisions are approved with some degree of independence. How does one get approval for something that appears on the face of it to make limited rational sense?

My colleagues and I joked in the past about how board rooms can be places *where great ideas go to die.* This is perhaps a tad unfair since it is not enough to have the personal conviction that a given decision makes sense; the originator needs to garner sufficient support to actually make it happen.

Some leaders have gravitas, others have charisma, some are just out-and-out experts in their field and garner instant respect. Successful leaders exhibit a raft of subjective, distinctly human traits that simply make them credible. Regardless of whether it's convincing cofounders of a bold new vision, raising capital from the equity markets, or engendering support from a board of professional nonexecutives - influence is critical.

It's easy to gain support for objectively sound propositions. The challenge is that, in most instances, such propositions will be uninspired. For the inputs and outputs in an investment case to be financially compelling, there can be very little risk and, thus, relatively limited upside. But imagine the sheer force of influence and conviction required to gain approval for a business case that defies convention. It takes vision on the part of the approvers, but more importantly, it comes down to the sponsor's credibility, and persuasive talents. Granted, some boards will have greater risk tolerance than others, but all of them know that their own reputations are on the line - a powerful motivator.

Whilst I have not had the priviledge of meeting either Musk or the late, Steve Jobs, I have worked with senior leaders in multi-billion-dollar companies for many years.

I was fortunate enough to speak with a former CFO of a FTSE100 company who is now on the board of several of the UK's leading organisations. As CFO, he presided over a famously demanding and charismatic leader. I recall hearing about the tears in the office when said CEO eventually left the organisation. They had vowed to protect employment at a time when many were cutting back staff and notoriously championed the view that profits sustain rather than define.

The company was relatively acquisitive during the CEO's tenure, reflecting rapid market consolidation and increasing digitisation. While the CEO and CFO were generally strongly aligned on potential acquisition targets, they disagreed on one particular transaction.

To coin the CFOs' parlance, it was *not a farm bet* (in the UK people often talk about *betting the farm*, a metaphor for making a high-risk decision). Despite having a multi-million-dollar ticket price, it was a risk that the company could afford to take as part of a balanced portfolio. For reasons possibly best known to themselves, the CEO was committed to acquiring the company despite a less-than-compelling business case.

The CFO made their thoughts known to the CEO in private. The latter was famously strong-willed and wished to proceed despite the exchange, having acknowledged and largely discounted the concerns. The CFO decided this was not a decision to die on the hill over. After the meeting, he sent a message to the CEO highlighting that he was prepared to support the deal but that, "he would eat his pants if it ever made any money." That was good enough for the CEO, clear endorsement from their finance partner! The two of them subsequently gained board approval, and the deal was completed.

It was, as anticipated, a flop.

I was perplexed as I listened to this account. Why would an experienced CFO responsible for safeguarding shareholder interests support something that they patently believed would fail?

The CFO knew full well that failing to back the initiative would burn his bridges with the CEO. He rationalised that it was a modest concession, and one that by supporting, would maintain his relationship with the CEO and keep his powder dry for decisions that really mattered in the future. Politics, or relationships, at the highest levels, are complex, and preserving one's right of veto for votes of consequence is an important part of building allyship and driving impact. Furthermore, there was always a chance that the CEO was right, they had been right many times in the past, maybe they were here. They had earned the right.

As we've highlighted not all decisions can be completely rationalised.

In the early 2000s, Amazon was known primarily as an online retailer. Imagine the resistance Jeff Bezos received when suggesting that the company create Amazon Web Services (AWS), offering cloud computing infrastructure to other businesses. The idea of a retail company venturing into enterprise IT services would have seemed illogical to many, particularly at a time when Amazon was famously struggling to turn a profit.

Whilst limited information is available about the methods employed by Bezos to garner support from the board, the result was stellar. AWS launched in 2006 and has since become a powerhouse, contributing substantially to Amazon's overall profitability and transforming the infrastructure market. The likes of Microsoft, Oracle, and IBM, who incidentally did not originate in retail, have subsequently struggled to regain market share.

High-stakes capital allocation decisions are not the only organisational choices that call for human talent. Almost anything related to other people requires a uniquely human touch. Unless or until robots take over, organisations are largely comprised of people organising affairs for other people. Granted, in digital-native organisations, there may be fewer people than in traditional stalwarts, but the principle remains.

You can objectively analyse a candidate from their CV and public profile and bolster this insight by talking to other people who know the individual in question. Fundamentally, though, as a hiring manager you must spend time with candidates to understand their likely fit.

Humans are supremely gifted at assessing other human beings. Throughout our evolution, it has been a critical survival technique. When we meet others, we make innumerable mental calculations which it would be impossible to rationalise. Within seconds, we start to form strong opinions. A first impression will have been made, and whilst most hiring managers are professional enough to retain an open mind, in a 60-minute interview, it's surprising how important a role intuition and gut feel play.

Given that organisations are at least in part determined by the strength of their people, finding leaders who can build and cultivate strong teams is another source of sustainable competitive advantage. Organisations should absolutely invest in technology to eliminate bias in the hiring process, but never to the point where experience and judgement become overruled by algorithmic logic.

One of the things that continues to amaze me, for example, is that industry leaders talk about the war for talent. A shortfall of people with the requisite skills and experience to propel their industry forward. Most, however, think linearly. If you keep looking at the same sources, in the same markets, and with the same demographics, you are going to seriously limit the gene pool available to the organisation. In a world where remote working is commonplace, and diversity valued, why are so many companies continuing to adopt traditional recruitment practices?

The Ultimate Black Box

Of course, the approach advocated above has challenges. The single biggest issue being that human judgement is hugely subjective. Because judgement requires subjective factors that can be hard to rationalise, such decisions are risky in high-stakes situations.

HBR reports that 70-90% of mergers and acquisitions fail[33], while

33 CHRISTENSEN, C. M., ALTON, R., RISING, C. & WALDECK, A. R. The New M&A Playbook. 2011.

McKinsey highlights that only around a third create value.[34] The fact that the latter, along with other major consulting firms, appear to be a consistent variable in unsuccessful M&A activity is perhaps a topic for another time.

As we have highlighted, one of the biggest challenges with technology is maintaining explainability and transparency when using so-called black box technology. The reality, however, is that the human mind is perhaps the ultimate black box.

Intuition, gut feeling, and judgement are hard to articulate. A track record and credibility built through demonstrable experience of making good judgements is important, but it is no guarantee of future success.

In the highest-stakes environments, the past is not a guarantee of future success.

Furthermore, it is precisely because humans are able to engender followership and influence others that close attention has to be paid to ensure that influence doesn't cross the line into manipulation. As we highlighted previously, agency conflict is a real issue within organisations. How do we prevent our strong-willed, charismatic, and highly persuasive leaders from making decisions that are more in their own interests than those of the shareholder?

The reality is that there is no good answer to the dilemma. It is

34 BIERLY III, P. E., KESSLER, E. H. & CHRISTENSEN, E. W. 2000. Organizational learning, knowledge and wisdom. Journal of Organizational Change Management, 13, 595-618, MC-LETCHIE, J. & WEST, A. 2011. Beyond risk avoidance

perhaps ironic that while in the previous chapter, I was able to highlight six relatively practical ways of ensuring that technology remains transparent and explainable, I can offer no equivalent method for managing human talent.

Strong HR policies can align incentive structures, but fundamentally, the board must perform their expected role with aplomb. As highlighted, data informs decisions, and it should not be overlooked. Receiving a board pack ahead of a meeting with limited time to review the provided information is never going to lead to optimal decisions. In a world where data dashboards put information on everyone's desktops, arguably, boards should be insisting on greater transparency and access.

However, such approaches will not overcome the fundamental challenge. In high-stakes decisions the less objectively certain an outcome, the higher the chance of a transformative result for good or bad. However, by automating decisions that are suited to machines, by investing in outstanding human talent, and by appointing engaged and professional boards, organisations can give themselves the best possible chance of success.

Summary: Talent Zone

Decision Zone Characteristics	Automation Strategy	Considerations
• Low volumes of data – including semi-structured and unstructured data • Low levels of data sufficiency – subjective criteria considered important in optimising outcomes	• Human judgement and experience highly prized – characterised by experts – invest in talent • Data used to inform decisions – invest in technology with caution, unlikely to differentiate	• Need to be cognisant of bias and systematic error • Decisions will, by definition, involve significant subjectivity • Data asymmetry likely to exist between decision maker and both board and shareholders • Trust plays critical role in driving outcomes • Exponential business outcomes may be achieved by creatively projecting the future

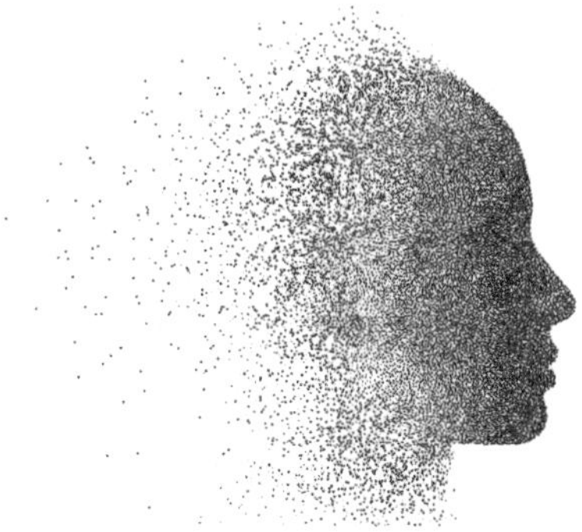

Chapter 10

A Model for Practice: Grey Zone

"Human plus machine isn't the future, it's the present. We must embrace this partnership to achieve things neither could do alone."

Garry Kasparov

~ Grey Zone ~

We concluded the previous chapter by acknowledging the challenge associated with exploiting human potential in our Talent Zone. Despite creating unique sources of competitive advantage by creatively projecting the future and influencing others, corporate history is littered with more cases of high-stakes failure than success.

Nonetheless, it is a challenge that organisations must embrace. Exploiting machines as coping pioneers where conditions allow creates the space for leaders to focus on those decisions that materially move the dial. There are challenges to overcome at either extreme of our model, but they serve as clear focal points.

This brings us neatly to the rather murky middle ground of our model. Where data volume/complexity and sufficiency are modest, we encounter what I've rather unimaginatively labelled Grey Zone decision-making, instances which are not ideally suited to either humans or machines.

As organisations navigate the intricate interplay between data-driven processes and human judgement, the Grey Zone presents opportunities and challenges that demand nuanced strategies and thoughtful leadership. This decision zone is, both literally and metaphorically, the largest of our three domains. However, it is a space that should be approached with caution and that is evolving rapidly.

Augmentation

At its core, grey-zone decision-making encapsulates scenarios where neither hard data nor automated processes alone can drive optimal decisions. Instead, these decisions necessitate a delicate balance of quantitative analysis and qualitative insights. When leaders talk about data-driven decision-making, many refer to this domain, where narrow use cases call for data insight overlayed with human judgement and experience.

A typical low-level business case is a great example of Grey Zone decision-making. Most organisations prescribe the format of supporting materials, deriving hard metrics such as NPV, payback period, and IRR. In theory, decision-making should be relatively straightforward. We have seemingly quantifiable inputs such as costs, expected returns, and a series of financial metrics that enable optimised decisions. These hard metrics allow ready comparison and prioritisation between business cases.

However, in reality, the inputs in such business cases are hugely subjective. An overly optimistic view of the potential market in one case, the ability to capture a disproportionate market share in another, and heroic cash flow projections in a third can heavily prejudice the relative comparison. In competition for scarce resources, experienced leaders have to assess and challenge the assumptions underpinning such projections. Whilst automation can help in the production of materials and the resultant financial analysis, the ability to effectively interrogate the human behind the business case is currently very much a soft skill.

The Grey Zone is typified by narrow use cases. Until relatively recently, almost all available technology was developed for specific, specialised domains. Moving between use cases and contexts was expensive and time-consuming.

Artificial General Intelligence (AGI) has long been considered the holy grail of automation. It envisions intelligent systems that can readily move between domains and use cases, using residual knowledge and adaptiveness to seamlessly address different contexts.

Human beings exhibit this adaptability naturally. I was talking with a CEO recently who described an interaction with his grandson in the context of our discussion on AGI. He'd shown his grandson how to spin a table tennis ball backwards by flicking his wrist and fingers. His grandson practised with the incessant fervour unique to children and was soon proficient. There was nothing particularly extraordinary in that.

Later that day, the same grandson was playing in the garden with a football. After he tired of kicking the ball around the garden, he picked the ball up and began spinning it backwards on the grass. On the face of it, there was nothing extraordinary there, either.

However, the ability to take a skill learned in one context with an object the size of a table tennis ball, and seamlessly move into an entirely different environment with a larger object, and apply similar principles is uniquely human. AGI aspires to replicate this ability in digital domains.

Whilst AGI may still be a distant promise, Generative AI has arguably begun to make significant inroads. Two years ago, when I was completing my thesis, I would argue that the Grey Zone very much dominated the technology landscape. Even where AI was emerging in practice, it was narrow.

However, LLMs such as ChatGPT have broad application with the potential to do everything from writing a poem to helping build a business case. The breadth of the data used to train such tools and the ability to respond to natural language prompts make the technology broader than ever before. Overlay the fact that downstream providers can quickly develop applications on top of core code, and you have highly versatile technology. Even if the technology cannot seamlessly move between certain contexts, the foundation models provided by LLMs make it far cheaper and more cost-efficient to address nuanced use cases.

Just last night I was talking with a commercial finance professional working within the property technology sector. They are building a solution to accelerate the speed of traditional residential property conveyancing. The idea is to use AI to sit across the end-to-end transaction, enabling standard questions to be answered automatically and support bespoke questions using natural language tools built on an LLM. It all makes sense. The vast majority of residential property transactional queries are relatively straightforward and readily automated.

As we were talking, it struck me that such a solution only a few months previously would have been impracticable to develop. Prior to GAI, such technology would have most likely taken the form of an expert system. The number of nuances in a property transaction would have made it very expensive and time-consuming to code. Certainly not impossible, but expensive. However, the combination of AI and machine learning inherent in an LLM, makes the solution much more economically and technically viable.

However, to my mind, it remains an example of Grey Zone decision-making. One of the biggest challenges in this space is the quality of land registry records and access to lease information, for example. When my wife and I last bought a property, a lengthy delay arose from working with poorly executed physical records outlining boundaries, lack of information over shared access rights, and even basic understanding of who owned title over a shared garage block. All proved expensive and time-consuming to resolve.

A machine is unlikely to resolve these issues any time soon and will continue to call for human augmentation. The ownership of the garage block in question, for example, was only resolved by the local estate agent's residual knowledge. Having been in the village for over 50 years – they knew the previous owner and were able to get them to sign over the rights to the block for the price of a bunch of flowers. While I don't doubt that machines can accelerate standard elements of the process, I question their ability to redress the edge cases. Time will tell whether the technology succeeds in appreciably accelerating the process and justifies a premium from consumers. I wish them luck.

In my own specialist domain, procurement, new technology is emerging at a rate of knots. However, it is narrow in application. Tools assist organisations in automating demand intake, using autonomous negotiation to drive savings on tail spend, and guiding users through the buying process for instance. However, such is the scope and relative maturity of each that organisational leaders struggle to stitch together specific tools to drive business outcomes.

One of the challenges with the Grey Zone is building an effective business case to support change. Fundamentally, technology either needs to increase the top line or help drive improvement on the bottom line. Few modern organisations are interested in driving efficiency for efficiency's sake.

The Grey Zone is notoriously challenging in this regard. In the foregoing example of procurement, if a tool enables an organisation to onboard suppliers more efficiently, reducing the associated effort of two full-time equivalents by 20%, then there simply is no business case. Either the organisation carries the cost of those individuals, or they don't – they don't suddenly become 20% cheaper just because technology has been introduced to do an element of their role. I've seen heroic business cases that tot up these percentages across a broad range of disciplines and teams, suggesting that the associated reduction will result in compelling financials. It is, however, a false economy. When it comes to business cases, companies should deal with absolutes, not hyperbole.

Any business case requires scale to generate returns. Building a case is straightforward if a traditional process is costly or inhibits revenue growth. Without scale, my advice would be to look elsewhere.

Narrow Use Cases & Change Management

Due to the high number of narrow use cases, organisations can easily find themselves investing in a significant number of pilots, resulting in what one executive referred to as *pilot paralysis*. A single organisation may have thousands of individual use cases. Whilst the investments in such technology may be modest, the narrowness of the scope and the sheer dilutionary impact of working simultaneously across so many projects can result in questionable financial and operational returns.

If organisations must invest in pilots in the Grey Zone, they should ensure a clear focus on high-potential use cases and avoid the trap of spread betting. Equally, it is important to ensure pilots have clearly defined parameters. What is actually being piloted and why? What are the success factors? Finally, if piloting with a technology vendor, sponsors should ensure that before they start the pilot, they understand the long-term commercial terms. Starting negotiations at the end of a successful pilot is never a smart place to be.

The second material challenge associated with this decision zone is that it is heavily reliant on human agents embracing technology. Change management is notoriously challenging when deploying technology and is particularly difficult in areas where humans and machines augment one another to secure business outcomes.

Where machines serve as coping pioneers, technology is likely to displace entire teams. The projects are not easy to implement, but on the other side of implementation, the technology is reliant on human agency to a very limited extent. In the Grey Zone, the operational success of a particular initiative will be as reliant on human agency as it is upon the technology itself.

The well-cited case of the Boeing 737 Max tragedy serves as a sobering reminder of what happens when automated, augmented decision-making goes awry.[35] A widely reported cacophony of errors with Boeing's new planes led to the death of 346 people across two flights in the space of a mere five months. In short, Boeing raced to launch their new planes, using an existing Federal Aviation Administration (FAA) certification to meet aggressive commercial timelines. However, existing credentials meant that the wings of the new plane could not be taller than those of its predecessor, resulting in the engines being placed further forward and materially altering the plane's aerodynamics. The result of the workaround was that it created unusual stall characteristics under certain conditions.

Rather than risk a lengthy recertification process by redesigning the compromised elements of the plane, Boeing developed an automated decision-making solution known as the Manoeuvring Characteristics Augmentation System (MCAS). The system used sensors to take corrective action in the event of predetermined stall conditions, which would push the plane's nose down and in theory correct the issue.

In the case of the Lion Air flight that tragically crashed on 29th October 2018, the plane reached a descent speed of 30,000 feet per minute, having descended sharply some 22 times during its ill-fated 12-minute flight. Subsequent investigation revealed that the pilots had not been informed about the potential stall issue or the MCAS system. Their lack of knowledge and training left them with limited ability to react to the catastrophic fault. Boeing had made certain

35 GEORGE, W. & MIGDA, A. 2020. What Went Wrong with Boeing's 737 Max? June ed.: Harvard Business School.

assumptions about the way pilots would react in such circumstances but had not tested the theory in practice.

By contrast, the pilots of the second flight, Ethiopian Airlines 302, which crashed on 9th March 2019, *had* been briefed on the MCAS system. However, when the system malfunctioned early into their flight, a raft of human errors exacerbated technical challenges in engaging the shut-off procedures and resulted in the death of all onboard.

An extreme example, but one that highlights the challenge of grey-zone decision-making and the challenges of putting a *human in the middle*.

Considered Deployment

Despite being the largest of the decision zones identified, organisations should avoid heavy investment. Technology in this decision zone is unlikely to materially differentiate or drive competitive advantage. However, it is all too easy to expend significant time, effort, and money on narrow use cases.

Summary: Grey Zone

Decision Zone Characteristics	Automation Strategy	Considerations
• Moderate levels of data – largely structured • Modest data sufficiency • Decisions require a mix of hard and soft decision making	• Avoid overly focusing on technology in this decision zone – poor return on investment against narrow use cases • Use case specific automation – may involve partial automation of process • Focus on high impact processes • Consider use of connected devices or digitisation to create future enablers to support high potential areas	• Care should be taken to avoid automating processes without tangible return • Avoid pilot paralysis and dilution across multiple projects • Automation strategy may result in resistance from impacted talent – consider change management strategy • Machines will augment rather than displace – may result in human in the middle – requires extensive training • Need to be cognisant of bias and subjectivity • Data asymmetry likely to exist

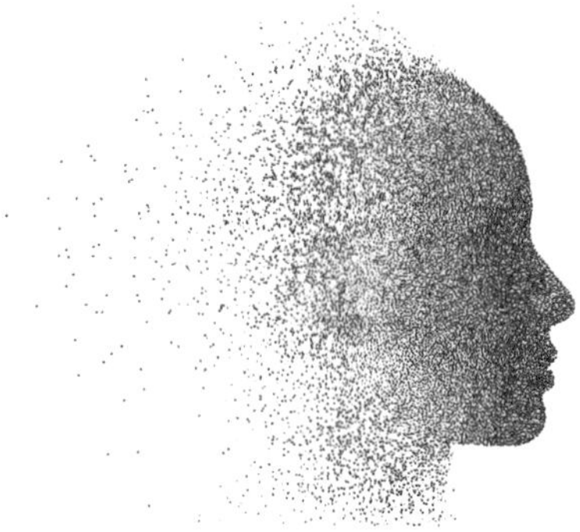

Chapter 11

A Model for Practice: Accelerators

"The pace of change has never been this fast, yet it will never be this slow again."

Justin Trudeau

~ Accelerators ~

Organisational leaders need to be thinking about *tomorrow's technology today* to stay ahead of the curve.

Large organisations tend to take a long time to make big decisions on technology, often considering only what is immediately in front of them. However, by the time leaders become comfortable with the associated technology, build an investment case, and undergo the invariably complex change and implementation programmes associated with deployment, they have often unwittingly deployed legacy technology.

Legacy debt is a huge issue for organisations trying to compete with agile new entrants. By legacy debt, we refer to the legacy technology and processes that typify large, traditional organisations. It is expensive and time-consuming to pivot, ceding advantage to the competition.

The world will continue to evolve at pace, with technology increasingly encroaching into both the Grey Zone and the Talent Zone. Four primary factors will drive that encroachment: connected devices, increasingly digital operations, synthetic data, and machine learning. We go on to explore each below.

Connected Devices – A World of Bits and Bytes

The expansion of connected devices has been nothing short of meteoric, with billions of connected devices in service across public and private domains. Increasingly every action, transaction, and interaction creates a potential data point. According to Forbes, the number of IoT-connected devices worldwide is projected to reach 25 billion by 2025.[36] These devices range from smartphones and wearable devices to industrial sensors embedded in manufacturing equipment and smart home appliances. Every device deployed collects data that businesses can leverage to derive insight.

In industry, connected devices are transformational, supporting precision agriculture through to optimised manufacturing of physical goods. In the former case devices monitor temperature, humidity, acidity and a raft of measures that can be refined to turn the notion of green fingers from an art to a science. In the latter instance, connected devices promote increased uptime by pro-actively monitoring equipment to allow preventative maintenance.

General Electric (GE), for example, claims to have saved customers $1.6 billion in lower operational and maintenance costs by deploying digital twins.[37] With over 1.2 million digital twins in place, from jet engines to wind turbines, GE uses predictive analytics to pre-empt issues, and test simulations in a safe environment. The digital twins

36 DE NIL, M. 2024. Connecting The Dots: The Future Of IoT In The Enterprise. https://www.forbes.com/councils/forbestechcouncil/2024/07/08/connecting-the-dots-the-future-of-iot-in-the-enterprise/: Forbes.

37 2024. Digital Twin Software. https://www.ge.com/digital/applications/digital-twin.

take feeds from sensors on the assets themselves and overlay such information with historical data and information from equivalent sources. Twins enable proactive maintenance to reduce unintended downtime.

In a like-manner Thames Water in the UK reportedly maintains 20,000 miles of water pipes - enough to circle the moon twice.[38] Deploying over one million smart meters, capable of delivering a twelve-fold increase in the number of active readings, has eliminated circa 80,000 leaks, saving 57 million litres of water a day!

Consumers, in turn, are contributing to this exponential increase in data. Wearable devices collect health and fitness data, providing users with insights into their physical activities and well-being. Similarly, we are increasingly driving electric vehicles, making ever greater use of smartphones, and sharing more information than ever before about our personal and professional lives on social media.

All of these factors lead to an explosion of data, and the trend does not look likely to abate anytime soon.

Capturing data is one thing for organisations; exploiting it is quite another. Data strategy is critical to the modern organisation. A complex legal framework surrounds data collection, privacy, and exploitation. I remember well, for example, Facebook's early disclaimers stating that they owned user's personal data. Fortunately, the law in most countries protects the unwitting consumer from such

38 2023c. Thames Water surpasses 1 million smart meter installations. https://www.thameswater.co.uk/news/thames-water-surpasses-1-million-smart-meter-installations.

outright exploitation, but the challenge for organisations is clear.

Historic contracts agreed with customers and consumers can hamper traditional businesses. Poorly executed disclaimers can prevent organisations from using historical data in a way that they might ideally like. Equally, the way in which such data has been stored and labelled can be a material inhibitor. Digital native organisations by contrast have the advantage of creating processes from scratch and typically adopt a data-centric philosophy from day 1.

I would argue that legacy companies struggling with their data strategy should not let their obsession with perfection prevent them from making tangible progress. It is very hard to redress the past, but relatively easy to ensure that the situation does not get any worse. I would always advocate for fixing the future state and then prioritising legacy remediation based on the prioritisation of high-impact use cases.

Synthetic Data

Had I written this book a mere six months ago, I would not have included commentary on synthetic data, largely because I did not know that such a thing existed at scale. In fact, I only discovered it following a recent chance invitation to a dinner with over 50 data scientists where the topic was discussed. However, the innovation looks set to turbocharge use cases that would otherwise be inhibited by quality training data.

Despite the incredible amounts of data available to train machines, the fact is that not all training data is created equally, and high-quality content is both in limited supply and potentially subject to copyright and other forms of intellectual property protection as we have noted. Synthetic data potentially redresses the balance.

Synthetic data is effectively training data produced by machines to train other machines. It can be produced on demand, in significant volume, and against exacting specifications.[39] In addition to overcoming issues related to sensitive information, the technology can help plug gaps in data, by creating idealised training sets.

As highlighted, a combination of both data sufficiency and data complexity/volume determines technology use cases. Where data sufficiency is high, but data is unavailable, the traditional method of redress would be to deploy sensors or otherwise collect the necessary information to plug the gap. Increasingly, synthetic data is being used to train algorithms in such instances. This method is particularly efficacious in medicine. Detection of lung cancer, for instance, would be inhibited without synthetic data to create a sufficient volume of scan images to train algorithms on.[40]

It's a fascinating evolution. We highlighted, for example, the COMPAS system used to support recidivism decisions in the US judicial system and its reliance on historically biased data sources. By using synthetic data, engineers would be able to create more representative, diverse training materials with the potential to drive enhanced decision-making.

Digital Operations – Driving Business Insight

39 TOEWS, 2022, Synthetic Data Is About To Transform Artificial Intelligence

40 SALEHJAHROMI, 2024, Synthetic PET from CT improves diagnosis and prognosis for lung cancer: Proof of concept

In parallel, organisations are increasingly digitising their operations, moving away from physical bricks and mortar and manual processes to digital platforms and automated workflows. COVID-19 arguably accelerated this shift, with organisations forced to accommodate smarter ways of remote working and servicing customers in an ever more digital manner.

Organisations have invested huge amounts of capital in reimagining their core enabling infrastructure from HR to finance. Each system and automated process flow creates data that can be exploited to drive greater insight into the business and improve decision-making. Customer interactions are now recorded in Customer Relationship Management suites; contracts are stored in ever more sophisticated smart repositories, whilst an individual's entire employment history is recorded in intelligent HR tools.

While such tools materially improve internal organisational efficiency, automated customer-facing tools drive an organisation's growth.

Domino Pizza is an excellent, if unlikely, example of such digital transformation. Founded in 1960 in Michigan, it has become one of the most successful fast-food franchises in history.[41] However, in 2008, the company was struggling, in light of an increasingly competitive market, and a product that, while highly rated on price, was derided by consumers (and a popular late-night chat show host) for flavour.

41 GROYSBERG, 2021, Tech with a Side of Pizza: How Dominos Rose to the Top

In the same year, the then-CEO, David Brandon, boldly decided to revisit the company's recipe, something it had resisted throughout its nearly 50-year history. In parallel, the company began investing heavily in technology. Domino's had historically retained a number of its own shops alongside its franchise outlets. The former allowed it to innovate in a way that would not otherwise have been possible.

Domino introduced a point-of-sale solution called PULSE, which it mandated across its outlets. Whilst not immediately popular with franchisees, the solution allowed customers to build their own pizza and track orders, providing effective inventory and staff scheduling. Customers could track their orders to a quoted accuracy of 40 seconds. Perhaps more importantly, the system provided data!

Having invested heavily in talent, Domino continued to innovate across its technology stack. They introduced a voice-controlled ordering aid called Dom in 2014, and, as early as 2017, piloted autonomous delivery units to address delivery staff restrictions. Their investment in technology enabled them to deliver to non-traditional locations such as baseball fields and beaches, whilst using Facebook and Instagram enabled them to marry technology and marketing seamlessly. One JP Morgan analyst observed that Domino was "a technology company disguised as a marketing company, disguised as a pizza company."[42] The numbers speak for themselves with Domino opening 1100 new stores in 2023 alone, generating circa $4.5 billion in revenue and recording record franchisee sales of over $18 billion dollars.

---

42 As reported by GROYSBERG, 2021, Tech with a Side of Pizza: How Dominos Rose to the Top

There is evidence of similar digital transformation across industries. The consequence of such technology-led change is that the volume and complexity of data is increasing rapidly. In the context of our model, this growth creates the environment for machines to increasingly serve as coping pioneers.

Machine Learning – Powering Data-Driven Decisions

Data, however, is meaningless without ways of making sense of it.

Machine learning (ML) has emerged as an essential tool for handling this data deluge. It enables organisations to extract valuable insights by discerning patterns undetectable by humans and do so at remarkable speed.

There is a dizzying array of machine-learning techniques available to engineers, and the landscape is evolving rapidly. There are three broad categories of machine learning, supervised, unsupervised and reinforcement learning, with a raft of derivatives within each. Whilst it's not important for most of us to understand the intricacies of such techniques, a rudimentary understanding of what method is being used to power algorithms within an organisation is important.

The risk profile associated with different techniques varies significantly, predicated on the degree of transparency and explainability that underpins a given model. Supervised learning, for example, uses relatively formulaic labelling within a training data set to determine desired outcomes from sample inputs. Relatively low risk. Reinforcement learning, by contrast, provides machines far greater latitude in determining how to achieve a particular goal by using reward signals to refine performance over time. The method is likely to result in more opaque systems.

Whilst I certainly wouldn't advocate for organisational leaders becoming quasi-data scientists, understanding the degree of transparency and explainability underpinning machine learning within proposed deployments is critical. Organisational leaders need to ask the question and recognise that there is a potential trade-off to be made. As highlighted by a report produced by Stanford University, black box solutions are outperforming more transparent models.[43] Conscious choices should be made, and suppliers should be probed on their methods.

Digital Worlds

You may recall that we highlighted in Chapter 4 a thesis written by Richard Dreyfus in the 1950s. To briefly recap, Dreyfus wrote an epistemological defence against the likelihood of machines encroaching into human domains based on his observation that humans, unlike machines, were perfectly adapted to large-world complexity as a result of being essentially grounded within it, and able to experience conceptual revolutions, enabling them to constantly learn from and reinterpret the world in context. Machines, by contrast, he argued, were abstracted and required engineers to translate physical reality into machine-readable code.

It's worth reflecting on this in the context of the above. In recent years the world has been increasingly translated into bits and bytes. The vast volumes of data we have just highlighted have created

---

43 Artificial Intelligence Index Report 2024. AI Index Report 2024 – Artificial Intelligence Index.

digital worlds, worlds where humans struggle and machines dominate. Machine learning enables software to undergo its own conceptual revolutions and to learn from experience. Autonomy and adaptability are narrowing the gap between organic and inorganic agents. Whether wittingly or unwittingly, we have created the conditions for machines to increasingly dominate.

I am looking forward to reading the first AI-generated draft of, *What Humans Still Can't Do*.

Exploiting Accelerators

Organisational leaders need to pay close attention to the accelerators we have identified. We highlighted the tendency for leaders to unwittingly focus on today's technology and attempt to exploit narrow use cases in the Grey Zone. Both are likely to result in poor return on investment and stagnation. Identifying accelerators can be a good way to force the organisation to think more progressively.

Organisations should consider the future data they need to make better decisions and drive growth. Investing in the relevant connected devices and digitising high-potential processes to collect data and exploit the same is a great way to gain a competitive advantage. Equally, considering whether this journey can be accelerated by using synthetic data is a question worth posing to technical teams. I rather suspect the latter is largely only being considered at present by data scientists and high-tech industries.

In a like manner, where data exists, but sufficiency is modest, organisations should consider what can be done to enhance and exploit insight. Machine learning should be considered, albeit with caution and a considered approach. Transparency and explainability are crucial, but the technology is important to consider.

Summary: Accelerators

Accelerator	Strategy	Considerations
Connected Devices	• Deploy sensors and connected devices to collect high potential data for exploitation by machines serving as coping pioneers	• Exploit high potential opportunities only • Robust data strategy required • Consider ethical and legal aspects of data collection and exploitation
Digital Operations	• Automate high potential business processes to drive efficiency and generate data insight	• Exploit high potential opportunities only • Robust data strategy required • Consider ethical and legal aspects of data collection and exploitation
Synthetic Data	• Consider use of synthetic data for high potential use cases where historic data is an inhibitor	• Consider return on investment - costly strategy • Robust synthetic data framework and foundations required • Avoid unintended design bias

Accelerator	Strategy	Considerations
Machine Learning	• Use of machine learning to increase data sufficiency and promote ability for machines to serve as coping pioneers	• Considered use of black box technology within robust ethical framework • Consider role of human oversight • Ensure explainability, transparency and clear decision logic for all but lowest risk decisions

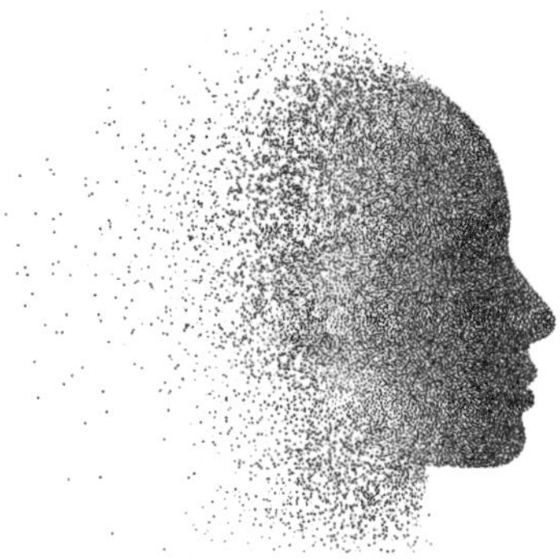

Chapter 12

A Model for Practice: Accommodation & Resistance

"Written laws are like spiders' webs; they will catch, it is true, the weak and poor, but would be torn in pieces by the rich and powerful."

Anacharsis the Scythian

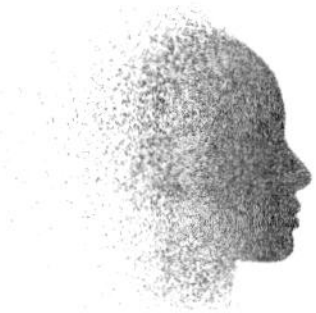

~ Accomodation & Resistance ~

While we can debate how quickly machines will encroach into human domains, the fact that they will increasingly be capable of performing tasks previously confined to organic agents is beyond doubt. Machines, however, will face both accommodation and resistance from various forces, which we go on to explore in this chapter.

Legislation – Balancing Risk & Innovation

Legislation will undoubtedly play an important role in determining the ethical and responsible parameters governing machines, particularly AI. Deploying organisations will look to legislators to establish appropriate boundaries and protect their interests.

However, governments face a difficult balance between encouraging innovation and managing risk. At the time of writing, this is perhaps one of the more interesting debates to follow as it continues to unfold.

Regimes in different parts of the world are adopting very different approaches to legislating AI and associated technologies, and the situation is evolving rapidly. Restrictive legislation is likely to push innovative solution providers to more progressive shores, restricting the technology available in the associated markets.

Given the propensity for technology to generate wealth and bolster the economy, restrictive policies are likely to be unpopular with capitalist voters and bleeding-edge organisations.

By contrast, pro-innovation legislative regimes will gain faster access to innovation, but governments risk failing to protect their citizens. Existing laws protecting privacy, copyright, human rights, and other legislative frameworks will certainly help prevent some of the worst potential abuses, but they do not go far enough. AI is creating unique risk profiles.

As ever, technology risk can be considered on a spectrum. At the most extreme end of this spectrum, there are concerns regarding existential risks associated with AI. Commentators warn of dystopian-like futures and the risk of scenarios previously confined to the pages of science fiction novels. How do we ensure that we build sufficient safeguards to prevent a Terminator or Matrix-like scenario where machines rise up against their creators? Far-fetched? Maybe, maybe not. The fact that California legislators advocate for a *kill switch* and that staff at OpenAI warned about the risk of frontier technology in an open letter[44] suggests that it merits closer attention.

Many influential figures, including Elon Musk, have warned of the potential unintended consequences of allowing technology providers free reign. Interestingly, in the latter's case, it does not appear to have prevented him from throwing his weight behind various bleeding-edge AI initiatives! The same can be said across

44 FIELD, H. 2024, Current and former OpenAI employees warn of AI's 'serious risks' and lack of oversight, https://www.cnbc.com/2024/06/04/openai-open-ai-risks-lack-of-oversight.html

the high-tech industry. There appears to be a marked difference between *saying the right thing* and *doing the right thing*. As David Evan Harris noted in his recent written testimony to the United States Senate, "when one tech company tries to be responsible, another, less responsible one steps in to fill the void".[45] Thus, unless and until all such companies are effectively governed, none of them will volunteer to slow the pace in isolation.

As a recovering philosopher, I find this debate particularly fascinating. In I Robot, Isaac Asimov introduced three laws of robotics:

1. First law: a robot may not injure a human being or, through inaction, allow a human being to come to harm.
2. Second law: a robot must obey the orders given to it by human beings except where such orders would conflict with the first law.
3. Third law: a robot must protect its own existence as long as such protection does not conflict with the first or second law.

Whilst it is obviously a fictional account, I would argue that some form of basic ethical framework needs to be thought about and encoded into advanced AI.

However, considering the principles that should underpin autonomous machines is trickier than you might first imagine. The first principle above, for example, could potentially result in failing to harm one individual at the expense of a million. The definition of

45 HARRIS, D. E. 2024. Written Testimony of David Evan Harris. https://www.judiciary.senate.gov/search/?q=carter%20 page&page=4&pagenum_rs=9: U.S. Senate on the Judiciary Subcommittee on Privacy, Technology, & the Law.

what constitutes *harm* is also ambiguous, and so it goes on. With the drive towards agentic AI gathering pace, these types of questions will become increasingly pertinent.

Although we need to return to more immediate practical concerns, while we are in the realms of the existential, it is worth highlighting a comparison between AI and the arms race in the 1940s.

I recently watched the Oppenheimer movie and was gripped, so I went on to read American Prometheus. What struck me most was the similarity between the nuclear arms race and the emergence of AI. Well-intentioned scientists and engineers raced to develop a technology that was poorly understood, and the unintended consequences of which could not have been foreseen. Driven by the knowledge that it was a high-stakes race to develop the weapon ahead of the competition, any thought of whether such technology should be developed, was circumvented by the drive to get there first. Once developed, it could never be undone and the lasting consequences of which are all too familiar to us.

It is very easy to draw parallels with our current predicament regarding AI. In this instance, the technology is being driven by powerful commercial incentives and will reside in private hands. Competitive forces are driving engineers to go further and faster than their rivals. Again, with each evolution, it is impossible to go backwards, and advancement becomes the new norm. Whilst consideration is being given to how to develop such tools responsibly – there is little evidence that such considerations are having a material effect. The unintended consequences of this commercial race are perhaps even less predictable than those associated with the arms race and even harder to undo.

Despite reluctance from many to entertain dystopian futures and to *fearmonger*, it is a debate that requires greater attention than it is currently receiving. It is not, in my opinion, fearmongering to rationally discuss a potential outcome, even if only to get comfortable with the fact that it can be discounted.

While it's a fascinating debate, we need to return to more immediate, practical concerns. While existential risks may be very real in the *near future*, social scoring, invasion of privacy, copyright infringement, discrimination, and restricted access to essential services are all very real risks *now*.

Copyright, for example, is an interesting case in point. LLMs have been trained on huge data sets. Does the use of such data constitute an infringement of third-party intellectual property? The residual information maintained by such systems is used to respond to prompts and, in some instances, to provide verbatim responses, limiting the need for the user to access an author's text directly. If you reflect on our discussion regarding the music industry, the comparisons should be clear. Given that LLMs would be unable to function without having used third-party content to train their systems, should compensation be payable to rights holders?

Emerging Legislation

As I write, the EU AI Act has been in force for several months, having come into effect on 1st August 2024. It is by far the most comprehensive piece of legislation issued anywhere in the world. However, it is hugely complex and, by the Commission's own admission, hard to operationalise. The EU, however, is not known for shying away from complexity with legislation – the General Data Protection Regulation (GDPR) and the existing harmonisation laws provide ready examples.

The Act serves as an interesting marker. The proffered definition of AI is of particular note. It may sound like a very trivial point in a piece of legislation that extends over hundreds of pages, but it is the lynchpin on which the rest of the Act is based. Other legislative regimes (including the UK) have stopped shy of defining AI, which feels like a significant omission. Although we have talked about AI throughout these pages, and we likely all have an intuitive understanding of what AI is, how should we define it for legislative purposes? The EU definition is a very good start.

The definition extends to a mere 54 words but is loaded with meaning. I include it verbatim below owing to its importance in laying a foundation for others to follow:

> "'AI system' means a machine-based system that is designed to operate with varying levels of autonomy and that may exhibit adaptiveness after deployment, and that, for explicit or implicit objectives, infers, from the input it receives, how to generate outputs such as predictions, content, recommendations, or decisions that can influence physical or virtual environments."[46]

The definition takes a few readings and, as ever, is open to interpretation. My own interpretation is that the definition hinges on

46 https://artificialintelligenceact.eu

the fact that AI uses *inference* to make recommendations and decisions, acts with *autonomy* and is capable of exhibiting *adaptiveness* over time. Machine learning is inherent in the definition, given that it is the engine that allows inference and adaptiveness. The ability to influence physical and virtual environments feels like a truism for technology generally and offers little by way of differentiation.

So, we have a definition that points to an inorganic agent that makes decisions and recommendations based on implicit rules, can act autonomously and has the potential to evolve over time. In other words, the Act is intended to govern an impressive piece of kit!

Since the launch of ChatGPT and the advent of GAI, providers have been clambering over themselves to rebrand their solutions as AI. Many are a long way removed from the foregoing definition and are more accurately described as smart automation. That's not to detract from the solutions, merely to suggest that informed buyers need to cut through the hyperbole. The Act may help. It provides a clear definition, and the consequences are material. I look forward to challenging providers so armed. I suspect far fewer suppliers will want to jump on the AI bandwagon once the Act's provisions begin to bite.

The Act adopts a risk-based approach. It is focused on ensuring that providers and deployers of AI technology respect fundamental human rights and safety concerns. It prohibits certain activities (social scoring, real-time remote biometrics, exploiting vulnerabilities, and manipulation), while the majority of provisions are aimed at governing high-risk systems and general-purpose AI, particularly those with systemic risk. Systemic risk refers to those AI systems that represent a moral hazard owing to the amount of compute used in their training and the breadth of their potential application. The Act is underpinned by relatively material penalties.

As an indication of the challenge facing organisations, OpenAI has claimed to have the technology to watermark AI-generated content but is reluctant to release the same fearing negative impact on user numbers. Although the Act mandates such provisions from August 2026, I rather suspect that by that point, the world will have moved on and watermarking content will be shutting the stable door after the horse has bolted.

Whilst the EU Act is a great start, it is clear that legislation cannot hope to keep up with the pace of the technology it seeks to govern.

The Act was at least three years in the making (the Commission published a proposal to regulate AI in the EU in April of 2022) and will be gradually operationalised over the next 36 months. Think about that for a second. The origination of the Act predates the public release of ChatGPT by several months, an impressive piece of foresight and forward thinking. However, in the mere two years since its release, ChatGPT, and GAI generally, have spawned an entire industry, whilst the legislation has yet to have any material impact. As we've just highlighted, watermarked content will not be mandated until almost two years after the act was published.

Further, the very fact that even those who are currently engaged in prohibited practices have six months to cease such activity is of concern. Why do such obligations not take immediate effect? Surely if a given activity merits prohibition, it should take immediate effect. Perhaps even more worryingly, in other regimes, such practices are still permitted.

According to a recent report by Stanford University, The AI Index reported that 32 countries have enacted at least one AI related bill, bringing the total to 148. For a nascent industry that's a dizzying number. This is going to be a complex area of law and practice.[47]

To do full justice to the topic of responsible AI would require a lengthy book in and of itself. However, leaders should be aware of the ongoing dialogue and debate. This should not be the exclusive domain of lawyers and engineers. Nor should leaders imagine that because the legislative obligations largely sit with providers, they are protected. The practical and commercial risk will, as ever, sit largely with deploying organisations. Organisations need to be thinking about the potential liabilities and protecting their own staff, data, and reputations *now*. Waiting for legislation to catch up is not a sensible approach.

With all that said, legislation will also serve to *accommodate* technology.

It's a slightly perverse notion to consider legislation as accommodating disruption. However, clear parameters will help legitimise activity. For many organisations understanding the realms of the permissible and having clear guidelines regarding safeguards encourages innovation and enables machines to move into the mainstream. The sheer fact that legislation points to what is permissible motivates organisations to push towards the extremes, knowing that if they don't, the competition likely will.

---

47 Artificial Intelligence Index Report 2024. AI Index Report 2024 – Artificial Intelligence Index.

Evolving Customer Attitudes

Outside of legislature, customer attitudes are going to play a significant role in the future of technology.

The world is becoming increasingly dehumanised. By way of example, my grandmother recently celebrated her 100th birthday. Amongst the messages she received was a card from her former bank manager. The same bank manager has sent her a Christmas card every year for over forty years. Such a gesture harks back to a time when personal relationships with customers mattered.

My grandparents used the same high-street bank in London for most of their lives and came to know the staff and manager well. Contrast that experience to modern-day banking. It's actually pretty challenging to speak to a human being at all, with the high-street experience largely automated and most of us opting to perform the vast majority of functions online. The last thing that took me to a physical premises was the cheque that the same grandmother sent me each year on my birthday (£1 for each birthday I have celebrated). Now that I can deposit said cheque digitally, I have no occasion to visit a branch, even if it were possible to find one.

Until relatively recently, credit decisions were made by actual human beings, albeit informed by data. I remember sitting down with a mortgage advisor when my wife and I were buying our first joint property. It was a financial stretch, but we could make it work by taking advantage of a graduate mortgage scheme.

After reviewing the *physical* paperwork and providing *physical* evidence of employment, salary, etc., our mortgage was agreed in principle. Subsequently, we made an offer on a house and celebrated that evening when the offer was accepted.

The following day, the bank contacted us to advise that, unfortunately, we were not eligible for the graduate mortgage we had been offered. I forget why. My wife was both furious and upset. Cue angry phone calls with the manager of the local branch. There were tears and a lot of angry, frustrated words. The manager was hugely apologetic, and in fairness to them, they went away and fixed the problem. They agreed to extend the originally proffered arrangement. We spent ten years living happily in the resultant property.

Nowadays, that simply would not happen. Most credit decisions are made online, and decisions are pretty much final. Even if you could speak to a human being, they have relatively limited authority to act outside of policy. This is, of course, less true, the wealthier one becomes. The more money that is at stake, the more likely one is to deal with an actual person and the greater the degree of latitude that is likely to be extended.

The same is true of medical support. Rewind a few years, and the default process was to visit the GP surgery and seek advice from a doctor you knew reasonably well. A good doctor assesses a situation from the moment you enter the room. A countless number of physical cues relay information to an experienced physician ahead of any description of the ailments being relayed. Nowadays, the first port of call is an online assessment.

While travelling in Australia recently, I availed myself of a virtual GP. It was efficient, but fundamentally relied on my ability to describe an issue with my arm in the absence of the physical manipulation that would ordinarily be performed by a physical doctor. Having received no relief, I visited a physiotherapist. The professional in question spent a significant amount of time understanding what had led to the injuries and discerning my recent lifestyle choices. Needless to say, the result was far more impactful, and the exercises I left with had an immediate impact.

Skip forward a few more years, and it's not too wide a stretch to imagine that you won't have to visit a GP at all. Your wearable device will relay information concerning your health, sleep patterns, and fitness to a digital GP. When your blood pressure, cholesterol, or other health indicators increase, you will be proactively contacted, and suitable medication will arrive without prompting. An efficient but completely dehumanised experience.

I could write at length about the transition from physical to digital, but the key issue is simply customer tolerance for change.

Younger generations born into the digital age exhibit greater comfort and adaptability with technology than older generations. Given that digital natives have never known any different and have grown up valuing digital relationships and convenience, we can expect generational attitudes to continue to shift in favour of automation.

The extent to which this transition will be accommodated remains to be seen. While we are unlikely to see automated teachers in classrooms or digital judges in courtrooms anytime soon, customers' accommodation and resistance should not be underestimated as a driver/inhibitor of technology.

Regulatory Bodies

Regulatory bodies have always played a critical role in the practical application of law within their domain-specific areas. This looks set to continue, with many worldwide governments adopting a risk-based view on governing AI and associated technologies. Regulators are well-placed to understand such risks in context.

In the UK the government's *pro innovation approach to AI*, devolves considerable authority to regulators within their respective industries. Whilst the UK has elected not to issue mandatory legislative measures or even to define AI, it is looking to regulatory bodies to determine appropriate measures to ensure that the core tenets of its framework are implemented effectively. Whilst not wholly dissimilar from the measures we proposed in Chapter 8, the UK framework centres around safety, security and robustness; fairness; appropriate transparency and explainability; accountability and governance, together with contestability and redress.

Most leaders that we spoke to operating within heavily regulated industries spoke positively of the roles of the regulators and their close working relationships. In the UK's case it will be interesting to see how the circa 90 regulatory bodies strike an appropriate balance in light of the self-proclaimed pro-innovation approach. The fact the UK has not even troubled itself to define AI, suggests that regulators have their work cut out for them in the coming months. Their attitudes are likely to have a material impact on the speed and breadth of adoption.

Professional Bodies – Protecting Traditional Professions

Given generational shifts, we might argue that we will not save ourselves from ourselves, whilst legislation will be too glacial to make a material impact. Perhaps a surprising last defence for some may come from professional bodies.

In the context of white-collar professions such as law, accountancy, and medicine, professional bodies have long served as gatekeepers, setting standards and overseeing conduct to ensure the integrity and reliability of their fields. These institutions have historically wielded significant influence, often erecting barriers that protect their domains from technological disruption. While this guardianship maintains quality and ethical standards, it also presents barriers to more innovative solutions.

In the US, for example, it is illegal to practice law or provide legal advice without a qualified lawyer. The emergence of platforms like LegalZoom, which offer online legal services without the direct involvement of qualified lawyers, exemplifies the friction between disruptive technology and established professional standards. LegalZoom operates in a grey area and the risks for LegalZoom are substantial. Any misstep could result in significant penalties and even jail time.

Ironically, as I was writing this section a news alert flashed up on my screen highlighting that the Top 10 UK law firms have increased fees by 40% in the last five years.[48] Clearly, such firms have managed to exploit rampant inflation in recent years. However, it feels like a strange dichotomy to me. At a time when we are actively moving towards an environment where consumers and customers can increasingly self-serve, it seems perverse that such firms are continuing to thrive. I suspect, however, that informed customers will increasingly push back, and greater use of technology will reduce reliance on all but the most nuanced support.

Parallel resistance is evident in the finance sector, particularly within accountancy. Whilst accountants don't benefit from the type of protection enjoyed by lawyers in the US, accounting standards have evolved to a point where they are "not necessarily common sense anymore" and demand "significant judgment" to interpret. This complexity curtails the immediate adoption of fully automated decision-making systems as automated tools struggle to navigate the nuanced nature of modern accounting practices.

In medicine, the adoption of AI-driven diagnostic tools faces similar hurdles due to stringent regulatory standards and the paramount importance of maintaining patient safety and trust. While these protections are essential for safeguarding quality, they also slow the pace at which technology can be adopted and scaled.

Summary: Accomodation & Resistance

It can be easy to get carried away with technology at present, but it is

---

48 ROGERSON, P. 2024. Top 10 UK law firms increase fees by 40% in five years. https://www.lawgazette.co.uk/news/top-10-uk-law-firms-increase-fees-by-40-in-five-years/5121258.article: The Law Society Gazette.

worth paying attention to those factors that will curtail encroachment.

Factor	Considerations
Legislation	• Legislation struggling to keep pace with the technology it seeks to govern and challenging to operationalise • A spectrum exists between risk aversion and pro-innovation. For those launching technology, a considered market approach is critical • Organisations cannot afford to default to technology and should take active measures to protect their interests in relation to immediate commercial challenges • Existential risks should not be overlooked – but are of less immediate practical concern for the majority of leaders • Harmonised legislation looks unlikely – calling for country specific approach
Customer Attitudes	• Customer tolerance of dehumanised experience looks set to continue with younger generations valuing convenience • Older generations are likely to be more reluctant to embrace technology at the extremes • Attitudes should be monitored and not taken for granted
Customer Attitudes	• Something has been lost in the digitisation of certain services, and organisations should consider whether reintroduction may command a premium

Factor	Considerations
Regulators	• Will play an important role in regulated industries • In certain markets, UK included, regulators will define standards in the absence of specific legislation • The landscape will be very complex – the UK alone has 90 regulators
Professional Bodies	• Professional bodies look set to continue to protect traditional professions, including law, accountancy, and medicine • Accommodation is likely to emerge as consumer and customer habits shift • Professions will either need to disrupt themselves or see continued encroachment from new entrants

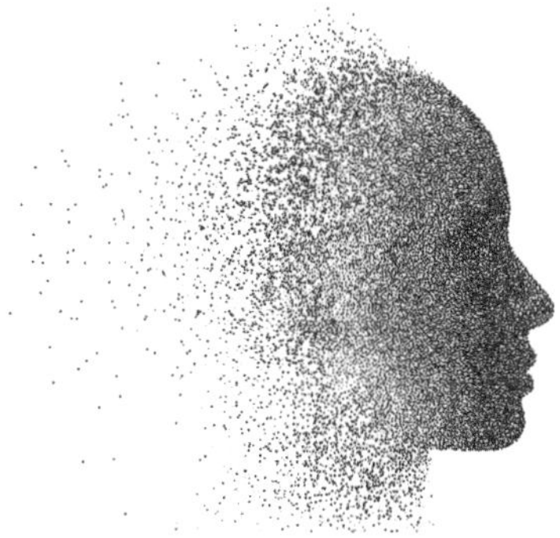

Chapter 13

A Look to the Future

"The future belongs to those who prepare for it today."

Malcolm X

~ A Look to the Future ~

Someone once told me that the future is *easy to imagine but difficult to believe.* In hindsight, I think this understates the challenge. It is becoming increasingly difficult even to imagine the future, let alone believe it.

The world will continue to change in unpredictable ways as the compound impact of exponential progress continues to bite. As I write, I've just finished watching a video clip in which Satya Nadella, the CEO of Microsoft, suggests that Moore's Law has been overtaken by scaling laws which will see technology progression double every six months.

It's hard to disagree with Nadella's assertion. It's fast and furious at the moment, but it's only going to get faster. This week's big reveal was that agentic AI can now control a user's machine for the first time. By the time you read this, it will already be old news.

To compound this, quantum computing looks closer than ever before. Without digressing too far, quantum computing is capable of encoding data using qubits, as opposed to traditional computers, which rely on binary. I don't pretend to understand the science behind quantum computing fully. I do, however, know that, unlike a bit, quantum qubits can store data exponentially, "two qubits can compute with four pieces of information, three can compute with eight, and four can compute with sixteen".[49] According to IBM, quantum is estimated to become a $1.3 trillion industry by 2035. If anything, that number feels understated.

Whether Artificial General Intelligence will become possible in that future remains to be seen. But, as we stated at the outset of this book, the world will soon look very different regardless of the exact nature of technological advancement. The only real question is *how* different it will look.

As an example of the dystopian future we are headed towards, I wonder how many people have heard of synthetic legal entities.

Cast your mind back to our discussion on organisational theory. I highlighted that organisations are legal fictions, separating a metaphysical entity from its owners and managers. Well, imagine for a second that the metaphysical entity was no longer metaphysical. Imagine that the legal entity itself was powered by advanced AI. What would an AI-powered synthetic organisation look like? How would it allocate roles and decision-making responsibility between other machines and human talent, and would it consider the latter necessary at all?

Most of us find it difficult to imagine such a future, but is it really such an outlandish idea?

Could an entirely synthetic business become possible in a world

---

49 IBM, 2024, https://www.ibm.com/topics/quantum-computing#:~:text=A%20qubit%20can%20behave%20like,forward%20for%20certain%20important%20problems.

with increasingly sophisticated AI? A synthetic legal entity with an entirely digital footprint, run for the benefit of shareholders (some of whom may well be machines) but with complete autonomy over operations and decisions. Such an organisation would massively reduce overheads. No staff, no premises, and no inventory. If you take high-frequency trading, for example, why could a synthetic model not potentially work?

What could possibly go wrong?!

Whether you believe such a future is likely or even possible doesn't really matter. Such thought experiments challenge us to step outside of our comfort zone and the immediacy of our day-to-day challenges to consider alternative futures. Creativity and imagination are important human traits that will be valuable in the brave new world.

Over the course of the last twelve chapters, we have taken a whistle-stop tour across a range of interconnected topics. I'll now attempt to draw these strands to a conclusion, at least of sorts.

We started by challenging the premise that humans are rational decision-makers. The purpose was not to suggest that decision-makers are incapable of rationality, merely that many of our decisions are made using intuition and instinct. As a consequence of our cognitive limitations, temporal restrictions, and lack of information, we typically make decisions that are good enough rather than optimal. Our inability to discern between System 1 and System 2 thinking can lead to bias and error.

There's no judgement involved in the foregoing summary, merely a statement of fact.

We then considered this reality against an emerging class of inorganic decision-makers. Tireless, impartial machines with access to increasing volumes of data and almost unlimited computing power. Such machines are capable of highly repeatable, rational decisions at scale.

I encouraged you to avoid labelling technology as far as possible, highlighting the hyperbole surrounding AI at present. Whether some of the emerging technologies are labelled AI, or not, is not hugely important. What is important is what the technology can do, and how they do it. The fact that no universal definition of AI exists should be proof enough to proceed with care.

From an organisational perspective, we recognised that decision-making is one of the most recurrent activities within organisations and a critical success factor. We discussed challenges associated with agency conflict and information asymmetry and questioned the extent to which shareholders are best served by managers making decisions that are satisfactory, as opposed to optimal. Fundamentally, I suggested that certain organisational decisions were perhaps better suited to machines, acknowledged the brilliance of certain leaders in high-stakes decisions, and recognised the need to strike an appropriate balance between the two.

The model for practice introduced in response to the foregoing observations recognises data's critical role in decision making, and its part in helping to strike a balance between machines and talent. The importance of data volume/complexity and data sufficiency cannot be understated, albeit they are relatively simple concepts to grasp.

Where both variables are high, machines serve as coping pioneers. Machines enable organisations to deal with scale efficiently while enabling pioneering insight from the associated data sets. Failure to exploit such conditions will likely lead to an existential challenge for laggards. High street banking was arguably disrupted by new entrants that saw the potential to deploy coping pioneers, reimagining the personal banking experience. While the former has recovered admirably, it serves as a pertinent reminder of the importance of remaining curious in a digital age.

The model also recognises the importance of elite human talent. Outstanding leaders are able to creatively project the future and positively influence others to make bold visions a reality. Such traits are uniquely human and difficult for competition to replicate. However, the subjective nature of such soft skills, can make it difficult to explain the basis for such high-stakes decisions, and significant degrees of trust are required by boards and shareholders to back such visions. It is a decision zone that calls for careful management but is a critical focus area.

We highlighted the murky area of Grey Zone decision-making between our two extremes. This zone is not perfectly suited to either machine or organic decision-making, calling for augmentation. It is typified by narrow use cases, poor return on investment, and can lead to pilot paralysis. More so than either of our other two zones, it calls for careful change management, training, and complex interactions between operators and machines. However, it is a space that is evolving extremely rapidly, driven by a number of accelerators that are seeing machines encroach from the boundaries of our model.

The number of connected devices and increasingly digital operations will continue to drive the number of scenarios where machines serve as coping pioneers, transforming the Grey Zone. The world is becoming increasingly reduced to bits and bytes, although in the near future, qubits may also play a role, in creating digital worlds.

Powered by machine learning and augmented by synthetic data, more and more use cases will succumb to machines. As technology becomes ever broader in application, and AI begins to transition more seamlessly between contexts, business cases will become more compelling with reduced outlays, accelerated time to value, and increased operational and financial impact. Traditional epistemological defences will gradually erode over time.

Organisational leaders need to be curious about these trends. It is not necessary to understand technology inside out. What is important is understanding where machines, connected devices, synthetic data, and machine learning can contribute to digital strategy.

Leaders should be looking ahead to the next wave of innovation rather than focusing on what is immediately in front of them. As technology accelerates, the risk of unwittingly deploying legacy technology increases. For most, avoiding the bleeding edge and being a fast follower will suffice – however, the emphasis in this context is on the word *fast*.

Legislation is likely to play an important role in determining the speed of adoption and providing assurance to nervous leaders. However, we have highlighted that striking a balance between promoting innovation and managing risk is weighing heavily on governments at present. The likelihood is that legislators will fail to keep pace with the technology they seek to govern and that, as such, organisations will need to take active, sensible steps to protect themselves. We point to transparency, explainability, data governance, privacy, fairness, and security & safety, as sensible parameters around which to build a responsible AI policy. Failure to do so could have significant consequences - both reputational and financial. In regulated industries, this may be slightly more straightforward, but in unregulated sectors, organisations will need to determine their own comfort zones.

Customer attitudes will play a role in shaping the future, but as we've highlighted, the tolerance of dehumanised experiences appears to increase with each successive generation. Whether this changes over time remains to be seen. Personally speaking, I can certainly live without having to deal with physical banking, but very much value physical teaching experiences, speaking to a GP in person, and dealing with an actual recruiter rather than an algorithm.

At the outset, I suggested that this book would offer no absolutes. However, there is perhaps one: machines will play a larger part in organisational decision-making going forward.

Whilst high-stakes decisions will always call for human talent, the number of instances calling for such input will reduce over time. Progressive organisations will continually scan the horizon, and actively consider their data, technology, and governance frameworks in light of the accelerators and inhibitors highlighted. The future of organisations will likely involve a modest number of decision makers, with technology creating the space for such talent to focus on those decisions that they are best suited to making, whilst technology quietly and efficiently deals with the rest.

The best leaders will look past hyperbole. They will not be swayed by dystopian hopes and fears. They will simply assess technology and human talent on its merit. They will be curious. Most importantly, they will prepare and act.

Annexes

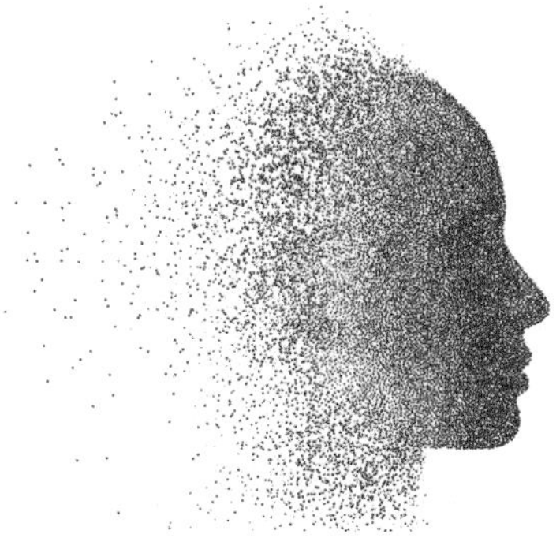

Annex I:

Practical Application

"In theory, there is no difference between theory and practice. But in practice, there is."

Benjamin Brewster

~ Practical Application ~

My greatest hope for this book is that it helps to inform thinking and frames some well-established debates in a practical way. Technology should not be the sole domain of engineers; in fact, AI has brought technology closer to the average business leader than at any time in the past. As such, it is important to be curious, prepare, and act.

The model we've covered together should help to frame discussions about technology, data, and human talent in a structured manner.

For those of you who are so inclined, the model can be used as a workshop aide to drive alignment and consensus amongst leadership teams.

Imagine, if you will, that you are a functional leader on an away day, thinking about your three-year plan. Somewhere in the agenda, there ought to be a session on people, processes, and systems. Using the model can be a great way to stimulate debate and engage the team in the future strategy.

I would start by making a list of all the decisions in the functional domain that reside with the team. One post per decision.

Draw the two axes we highlighted on a large whiteboard: data volume/complexity and data sufficiency.

Now invite members of the team to place each identified decision somewhere on the model. This is likely to stimulate debate, given that data sufficiency is somewhat subjective and likely to be challenged. That's no bad thing, as the debate is a useful way of driving alignment and highlighting challenging areas (these will almost certainly fall in the Grey Zone).

You should arrive at a populated model with decisions in each of the three decision zones.

You can now take each of your three decision zones and prioritise the decisions within them in terms of business or functional impact. Again, this should be done as a collective effort to drive alignment.

In the Automation Zone, group your decisions into system domains. In other words, how many of the decisions identified can be served by a common solution? If you don't know the answer to this in real-time, this can be done as a workshop follow-up. Find some volunteers who are curious and suitably motivated – it's a great opportunity to speak to suppliers in a structured manner. You should be left with the bones of a *systems strategy*.

In the Talent Zone, consider whether you have the right mix of talent in the team to support the critical decisions that sit within this space. Is the governance strong enough? Are there decisions that are being made particularly well or areas in which the team needs to be bolstered? Agree on a list of associated actions and follow-ups to redress the points raised. You now have the bones of a *talent strategy*.

The Grey Zone is perhaps the most challenging. For projects in pilot or proof of concept, actively question whether the investment is justified. Remember that the greatest benefit is likely to be derived from the two extremes of the model. The primary purpose of reviewing the Grey Zone is to minimise investment and find ways to push decisions into one of the two extremes.

Next, ask yourselves two distinct questions on data. What data do we have that we are not currently exploiting, and what data would we like but currently do not have access to? Put this on posts.

Use a separate model with the two data axes to start positioning your data posts. Where do they sit today?

Now consider where you would ideally like them to sit in the future. Draw arrows to illustrate.

Take two or three of the highest potential opportunities and discuss how you might move from your current state to your future state. What connected devices could be used to collect physical data, or what aspect of the operation could be digitised to create the idealised scenario you have identified? Could synthetic data help to plug the gaps?

Where the limitation is data sufficiency – consider whether there are ways of using technology to redress. Again, you may not know the answer in real-time, but it's a great takeaway for someone to follow up. What you have, though, is the start of a data strategy.

Finally, depending on your functional area, make a list of legislative constraints, customer attitudes, and any professional or regulatory body inhibitors that may prevent you from going further than you would otherwise like.

The outline above is simplistic but powerful. A great way of driving alignment by using a common model, highlighting the need to strike a balance between technology and talent, and starting to build a plan.

With appropriate preparation, I suspect that everyone involved will learn something and challenge previously held assumptions.

The final point to remember is that the world is dynamic. This should not be a *one-and-done* exercise but rather one that your team repeats at regular intervals, preferably at least once a year. The world changes quickly, so what may have been true twelve months ago may no longer hold valid.

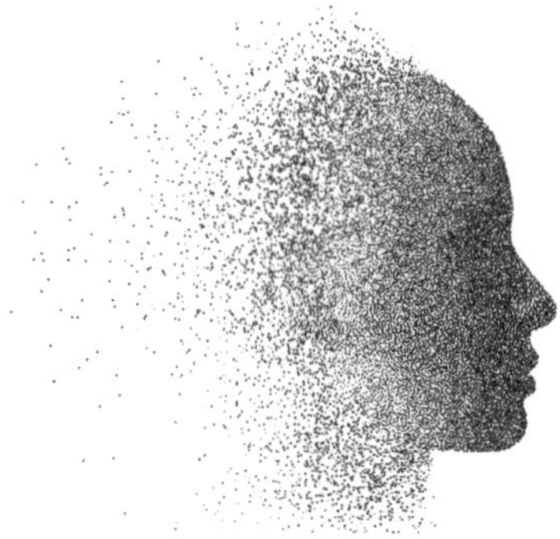

Annex II:

Writing & Publishing in the Age of AI

"Writing a book is an adventure. To begin with, it is a toy and an amusement; then it becomes a mistress, and then it becomes a master, and then a tyrant."

Winston Churchill

~ Writing & Publishing in the Age of AI ~

Given the nature of this book, it felt remiss of me not to talk about the disruptive influence of technology and GAI on the publishing industry.

Fortunately for me, ChatGPT and the myriad of other tools now available to aspiring writers, students, and academics only became available after the completion of my doctorate. Consequently, I was never challenged to decide how much to incorporate such tools into my final thesis. I was grateful for spell check and basic grammar correction, but that was about it. I've watched with fascination as educational institutions have grappled with the rapidly evolving landscape. The tools cannot be ignored, but how do students learn if the tools automate essential parts of the learning process?

That perhaps is a discussion for another day.

In parallel I've watched as authors have used the emerging tools to accelerate the rate at which they can create draft texts – both fictional and nonfictional. Certain online sources suggest that a portfolio of work can be produced in double quick time, with limited expense, and create compelling sources of passive income.

For my own part, I have been an active user of GAI since it became publicly available. When I say I've been an active user, I have often played with it rather than used it in earnest. I've been impressed by the quality of the prose, but not so much so that I would use it in place of my own (perhaps a tad arrogant, but I value the tone and voice of my writing). It is great for providing rapid information sources but needs to be constantly fact-checked. In short, I use it as a smart assistant.

As you might expect, my thesis was a dry and academically focused tome. At over 60,000 words, there are few that would be sufficiently motivated to read it. Yet I felt I had something that might be worth sharing, having spent nearly five years researching what has subsequently become a highly topical area.

GAI seemed to offer a shortcut to converting my work into something that could be published without inadvertently curing my reader's insomnia. The reality is, however, that I have used it relatively sparingly in the end. It can be great for generating examples to help bring key points to life, but the prose is less than inspiring, and whilst it serves as an excellent prompt, it does little more. It was great for finding the quotes I used at the start of each chapter, but again, I had to fact-check against the sources. In certain instances, it attributed quotes to the wrong individuals! I've been bemused at how often it has got facts subtly wrong. But, for all of its faults, it is still nascent. These teething issues will rapidly be resolved.

I found Grammarly of greater use than GAI. I enjoy writing and think I'm reasonably competent. You may, by now, heartily disagree. However, grammar has never been a strength. I found it interesting that using Grammarly to correct typographical mistakes and improve readability results in various online tools identifying original prose as being AI-generated. I'm yet to work out why that occurs, but it is interesting and unexpected. Equally, Grammarly now not only offers to correct basic grammar, but to rephrase sentences to make them more readable. That has caused me greater pause for thought. In various instances, the suggestions represent an improvement. It begs an interesting question: is a sentence redrafted by AI still the writer's original work? More to the point, does it matter?

I've discussed this with a few people and decided that *it depends*. A classic MBA response to pretty much every question ever posed! What I think is important is a writer's voice, perspective, and unique insight. Voice is an interesting notion. I suspect that those who know me best can recognise my writing style. Certainly, my long-suffering doctoral supervisor would be able to discern my unique way of expressing ideas. I would be loath to lose that, even if there were more grammatically accurate and compelling ways of making a point.

I've also been surprised, perhaps naively, at the nature of the publishing industry itself. Like many, I have always considered there to be a certain kudos associated with publishing a book. I was surprised, however, at how low the author royalties are despite relatively modest investment from the applicable publishing houses. Going from a draft manuscript to a published book can take well over six months, and in the modern age, the author is expected to do most of their own marketing.

Self-publishing, by contrast, results in the author retaining a far higher percentage of any resultant revenue, accelerating time to market, and retaining complete editorial control over the resultant product. Microservices are available to support every aspect of the process, from cover design to copywriting. That said, I decided to go it alone and learn how to use various tools myself. I've enjoyed the journey, although it would have been far quicker to use expert services.

My personal conclusion was that aside from being able to claim that you have had a book released by a professional publisher and some handholding along the way, I'm not entirely sure why the average author would decide to go that route.

So, there we have it. Whether good, bad, or indifferent, I have made nominal use of AI and decided to self-publish. That said, I think it will be a rapidly evolving industry, and I suspect that in the very near future, AI will be a significant force behind the best-selling literature.

References

2017. Wisconsin Supreme Court Requires Warning Before Use of Algorithmic Risk Assessments in Sentencing. 5 ed. https://harvardlawreview.org/print/vol-130/state-v-loomis/: Harvard Law Review.

2018. Justin Trudeau's Davos address in full. https://www.weforum.org/agenda/2018/01/pm-keynote-remarks-for-world-economic-forum-2018/: World Economic Forum.

2019. On AI, Analytics, and the New Machine Age, Harvard Business Publishing Corporation.

2023. A pro-innovation approach to AI regulation. https://www.gov.uk/government/publications/ai-regulation-a-pro-innovation-approach/white-paper

2023. As AI Improves, Investment in It Soars. Harvard Business Review, 101, 28-28.

2023. How responsible data can help us navigate the economic crisis. https://www.weforum.org/agenda/2023/01/davos23-responsible-data-protection-economic-crisis/: World Economic Forum.

2023. Thames Water surpasses 1 million smart meter installations.

https://www.thameswater.co.uk/news/thames-water-surpasses-1-million-smart-meter-installations.

2023. The State of Quantum Computing. Harvard Business Review, 101, 25-25.

2024. Digital Twin Software. https://www.ge.com/digital/applications/digital-twin.

AGRAWAL, A., GANS, J. S. & GOLDFARB, A. 2018. Prediction, judgment and complexity: a theory of decision-making and artificial intelligence. Working Paper 24243.

AGRAWAL, A., GANS, J. S. & GOLDFARB, A. 2019. Exploring the impact of artificial Intelligence: Prediction versus judgment. Information Economics and Policy, 47, 1-6.

AUTOR, D. H. 2015. Why are there still so many jobs? The history and future of workplace automation. Journal of Economic Perspectives, 29, 3-30.

AUTOR, D. H. & HANDEL, M. J. 2013. Putting tasks to the test: Human capital, job tasks, and wages. Journal of Labor Economics, 31, S59-S96.

BROOKE, J. 2017. Elon Musk Spends $1B In Developing Reusable Rockets.

https://www.scienceworldreport.com/articles/60085/20170623/elon-musk-spent-1b-developing-reusable-rockets.htm: Science World Report.

BRYNJOLFSSON, E. & MCAFEE, A. 2014. The second machine age: Work, progress, and prosperity in a time of brilliant technologies, WW Norton & Company.

BRYNJOLFSSON, E., MITCHELL, T. & ROCK, D. 2018. What Can Machines Learn, and What Does It Mean for Occupations and the Economy? AEA Papers and Proceedings, 108, 43-47.

CYERT, R. M., SIMON, H. A. & TROW, D. B. 1956. Observation of a Business Decision. The Journal of Business, 29, 237-248.

CYERT, R. M. M. J. G. 1963. A behavioral theory of the firm, Englewood Cliffs, N.J., Prentice-Hall.

DE NIL, M. 2024. Connecting The Dots: The Future Of IoT In The Enterprise.

https://www.forbes.com/councils/forbestechcouncil/2024/07/08/connecting-the-dots-the-future-of-iot-in-the-enterprise/: Forbes.

DREYFUS, H. L. 1996. Response to my critics. Artificial Intelligence, 80, 171-191.

DREYFUS, H. L. 2007. Why Heideggerian AI failed and how fixing it would require making it more Heideggerian. Artificial Intelligence, 171, 1137-1160.

EDMONSON, A. & JUNG, O. 2021. The Turnaround at Ford Motor Company. Harvard Business School.

EDWARDS, J. S. 1992. Expert systems in management and administration - are they really different from Decision Support Systems? European Journal of Operational Research, 61, 114-121.

EDWARDS, J. S., DUAN, Y. & ROBINS, P. C. 2000. An analysis of expert systems for business decision making at different levels and in different roles. European Journal of Information Systems, 9, 36-46.

EISENHARDT, K. M. 1989. Agency Theory: An Assessment and Review. The Academy of Management Review, 14, 57-74.

FREY, C. B. & OSBORNE, M. A. 2017. The future of employment: how susceptible are jobs to computerisation? Technological forecasting and social change, 114,254-280.

FRISCH, D. & JONES, S. K. 1993. Assessing the Accuracy of Decisions. Theory & Psychology, 3, 115-135.

GEORGE, W. & MIGDA, A. 2020. What Went Wrong with Boeing's 737 Max? June ed.: Harvard Business School.

GIGERENZER, G. & GAISSMAIER, W. 2011. Heuristic decision making. Annual Review of Psychology.

GIGERENZER, G. & GOLDSTEIN, D. G. 1996. Reasoning the fast and frugal way: Models of bounded rationality. Psychological Review, 103, 650-669.

HARRIS, D. E. 2024. Written Testimony of David Evan Harris.

https://www.judiciary.senate.gov/search/?q=carter%20page&page=4&pagenum_rs=9: U.S. Senate on the Judiciary Subcommittee on Privacy, Technology, & the Law.

KAHNEMAN, D. 2003. Maps of bounded rationality: Psychology for behavioral economics. American Economic Review, 93, 1449-1475.

KAHNEMAN, D., KNETSCH, J. L. & THALER, R. H. 2019. Fairness as a constraint on profit seeking: Entitlements in the market. Choices, Values, and Frames.

KAHNEMAN, D., SIBONY, O. & SUNSTEIN, C. R. 2021. Noise : a flaw in human judgement.

KAHNEMAN, D. & TVERSKY, A. 1984. Choices, values, and frames. American Psychologist, 39, 341-350.

KAHNEMAN, D. A. 2011. Thinking, Fast and Slow, 1st ed. New York : Farrar, Straus and Giroux, 2011

LEE, K.-F. 2018. AI superpowers: China, Silicon Valley, and the new world order, Houghton Mifflin Harcourt.

LOOMES, G. & SUGDEN, R. 1983. Regret theory and measurable utility. Economics Letters, 12, 19-21.

LOOMES, G. & SUGDEN, R. 1987. Some implications of a more general form of regret theory. Journal of Economic Theory, 41, 270-287.

ROGERSON, P. 2024. Top 10 UK law firms increase fees by 40% in five years.

https://www.lawgazette.co.uk/news/top-10-uk-law-firms-increase-fees-by-40-in-five-years/5121258.article: The Law Society Gazette.

SIMON, H. A. 1945. Administrative Behavior: a Study of Decision-Making Processes in Administrative Organizations (4th ed.). New York: Free Press.

SIMON, H. A. 1979. Rational decision making in business organizations. American Economic Review, 69, 493-513.

SIMON, H. A. & NEWELL, A. 1958. Heuristic Problem Solving: The Next Advance in Operations Research. Operations Research, 6, 1-10.

SUGDEN, R. 1985. Regret, recrimination and rationality. Theory and Decision, 19, 77-99.

TURING, A. M. 1950. I.—COMPUTING MACHINERY AND INTELLIGENCE. Mind, LIX, 433-460.

TURING, A. M. 2009. Computing machinery and intelligence. Parsing the Turing Test. Springer.

TVERSKY, A. & KAHNEMAN, D. 1974. Judgment under uncertainty: Heuristics and biases. Science, 185, 1124-1131.

WITT, S. 2015. How Music Got Free: The End of an Industry, The Turn of the Century, and the Patient Zero of Piracy. Viking PR.

ZEELENBERG, M. 1999. The use of crying over spilled milk: A note on the rationality and functionality of regret. Philosophical Psychology, 12, 325-340.

Printed in Dunstable, United Kingdom

67700547R00117